21.00

D0282712

THE LIFE OF 🦎 🦎 🦎 ROBERT LOUIS STEVENSON 🦎 🦎

BY GRAHAM BALFOUR
IN TWO VOLUMES WITH
PORTRAITS 🦎 🦎 🦎 🦎

I

PUBLISHED IN 🦎
NEW YORK BY
CHARLES SCRIBNER'S
SONS 🦎 🦎 1901 🦎

Republished, 1968
Scholarly Press, Inc., 22929 Industrial Drive East
St. Clair Shores, Michigan 48080

Library of Congress Catalog Card Number: 73-3152
ISBN 0-403-00143-9

CONTENTS

ILLUSTRATIONS

PREFACE

THIS book is intended to supplement the volumes of Stevenson's *Letters* already published. Originally it was to have been written by Mr. Colvin, and to have appeared simultaneously with the two volumes of correspondence, so admirably edited by him; but when health and opportunity unfortunately failed him, Mrs. Stevenson requested me to undertake the task. The reason for this selection was that, during the last two years and a half of my cousin's life, I had on his invitation made Vailima my home and the point of departure for my journeys, and, apart from the members of his own family, had been throughout that period the only one of his intimate friends in contact with every side of his life.

In Stevenson's case, if anywhere, the rule holds, that All Biography would be Autobiography if it could, and I have availed myself as far as possible of the writings in which he has referred to himself and his past experience. To bring together the passing allusions to himself scattered widely throughout his works was an obvious duty; at the same time my longer quotations, except in two or three manifest and necessary instances, have been taken almost entirely from the material which was hitherto either unpublished or issued only in the limited Edinburgh Edition. Whenever I found any passage in his manuscripts or ephemeral work bearing upon his life or development, I employed it no less readily than I should have used a letter or a hasty note, and in exactly the same fashion, regarding it as a piece of direct evidence from the best possible source.   Such use of documents, I need hardly point out, differs entirely from challenging admiration for the literary form of immature or unfinished compositions.   Where so much taste and discretion have been shown in preparing the final edition of his works, I should be the last to transgress the bounds imposed upon publication.

Since autobiography is wont to deal at some length with the first memories of its author, there seemed no occasion unduly to restrain this tendency in the case of the singer and interpreter of childhood, whose account of his early years is not only interesting in itself, but also of additional value for its illustration of his poems and essays.   Again, in the representation of his adolescence, it must be remembered that he never wholly ceased to be a boy, that much that belonged to him in early youth remained with him in after-life, and that enthusiasms and generous impulses would sweep in and carry him away till the end.

Much of course he did outgrow, and that almost entirely his worse part.   I feel that I should have done him a very ill service if I had refrained from showing the faults of the immaturity from which the character and genius of his manhood emerged.   He had many failings, but few or none that made his friends think worse of him or love him any the less.   To be the writer that he was, amounted to a great exploit and service to humanity; to become the man that in the end he became,

seems to me an achievement equally great, an example
no less eloquent.

Many persons, both friends and strangers to me, have
rendered my task far easier than I could have hoped.
There is hardly one of Stevenson's intimate friends but
has helped me in a greater or less degree, and if I were
here to repeat my thanks to all to whom I am indebted
for information, I should have to record more than sixty
names. Those to whom we owe most are often those
whom formally we thank the least; and to Mrs. Stevenson and Mr. Lloyd Osbourne I can never express my
indebtedness for their suggestions and their knowledge,
their confidence, their patience, and their encouragement. But, of course, for everything that is here printed
I alone am responsible.

The references to Stevenson's writings are necessarily
to the pages of the Edinburgh Edition, as being the
most complete English collection of his works.

LIFE OF
ROBERT LOUIS STEVENSON

CHAPTER I

HIS ANCESTORS

" The ascendant hand is what I feel most strongly ; I am bound in and in with my forbears. . . . We are all nobly born ; fortunate those who know it ; blessed those who remember."—R. L. S., *Letters*, ii. 230.

" The sights and thoughts of my youth pursue me ; and I see like a vision the youth of my father, and of his father, and the whole stream of lives flowing down there far in the north, with the sound of laughter and tears, to cast me out in the end, as by a sudden freshet, on these ultimate islands. And I admire and bow my head before the romance of destiny."—R. L. S., *Dedication of Catriona*.

" IT is the chief recommendation of long pedigrees," as Stevenson once wrote, " that we can follow back the careers of our component parts and be reminded of our ante-natal lives." [1]   But the threads are many and tangled, and it is hard to distinguish for more than a generation or two the transmission of the characteristics that meet in any individual of our own day.   The qualities that would be required by other ages and for other pursuits are often unperceived, and the same man might scarce be recognised could he renew his life in three several centuries, and be set to a different task in each.

[1] *Memories and Portraits*, p. 162.

1

Moreover, when any one has been dead for a hundred years, it is seldom that anything is remembered of him but his name and his occupation; he has become no more than a link in a pedigree, and the personal disposition is forgotten which made him loved or feared, together with the powers that gained him success or the weaknesses that brought about his failure. Therefore it is no unusual circumstance that, while we can trace the line of Stevenson's ancestors on either side for two and four hundred years respectively, our knowledge of them, in any real sense of the word, begins only at the end of the eighteenth century. After that date we have four portraits, drawn in part by his own hand, together with the materials for another sketch; and in these may be discerned some of the traits and faculties which went to make up a personality so unusual, so fascinating, and so deeply loved.

The record of his father's people opens in 1675 with the birth of a son, Robert, to James Stevenson, "presumably a tenant farmer" of Nether Carsewell in the parish of Neilston, some ten miles to the south-west of Glasgow. Robert's son, a maltster in Glasgow, had ten children, among whom were Hugh, born 1749, and Alan, born June, 1752.

"With these two brothers my story begins," their descendant wrote in *A Family of Engineers*.[1] "Their deaths were simultaneous; their lives unusually brief and full. Tradition whispered me in childhood they

[1] Except where it is otherwise stated, the quotations in this chapter and most of the facts about his father's people are drawn from the unfinished fragment of *A Family of Engineers*, printed in the volume of *Biography* in the Edinburgh Edition of Stevenson's works.

2

were the owners of an islet near St. Kitts; and it is certain they had risen to be at the head of considerable interests in the West Indies, which Hugh managed abroad and Alan at home," almost before they had reached the years of manhood.   In 1774 Alan was summoned to the West Indies by Hugh.   "An agent had proved unfaithful on a serious scale; and it used to be told me in my childhood how the brothers pursued him from one island to another in an open boat, were exposed to the pernicious dews of the tropics, and simultaneously struck down.   The dates and places of their deaths would seem to indicate a more scattered and prolonged pursuit."   At all events, "in something like the course of post, both were called away, the one twenty-five, the other twenty-two."

Alan left behind him a wife and one child, aged two, the future engineer of the Bell Rock, who was also destined to be the grandfather of Robert Louis Stevenson.   The widow was daughter of David Lillie, a Glasgow builder, several times Deacon of the Wrights, but had lost her father only a month before her husband's death, and for the time, at any rate, mother and son were almost destitute.   She was, however, "a young woman of strong sense, well fitted to contend with poverty, and of a pious disposition, which it is like that these misfortunes heated.   Like so many other widowed Scotswomen, she vowed her son should wag his head in a pulpit; but her means were inadequate to her ambition."   He made no great figure at the schools in Edinburgh to which she could afford to send him; but before he was fifteen there occurred an event "which changed his own destiny and moulded

3

that of his descendants—the second marriage of his mother."

The new husband was "a merchant burgess of Edinburgh of the name of Thomas Smith," a widower of thirty-three with children, who is described as "a man ardent, passionate, practical, designed for affairs, and prospering in them far beyond the average." He was, among other things, a shipowner and underwriter; but chiefly he "founded a solid business in lamps and oils, and was the sole proprietor of a concern called the Greenside Company's Works—'a multifarious concern of tinsmiths, coppersmiths, brassfounders, blacksmiths, and japanners.'" Consequently, in August, 1786, less than a year before his second marriage, "having designed a system of oil lights to take the place of the primitive coal fires before in use, he was dubbed engineer to the newly-formed Board of Northern Lighthouses."

The profession was a new one, just beginning to grow in the hands of its first practitioners; in it Robert Stevenson found his vocation and so entered with great zest into the pursuits of his stepfather. "The public usefulness of the service would appeal to his judgment, the perpetual need for fresh expedients stimulate his ingenuity. And there was another attraction which, in the younger man at least, appealed to, and perhaps first aroused a profound and enduring sentiment of romance; I mean the attraction of the life. The seas into which his labours carried the new engineer were still scarce charted, the coasts still dark; his way on shore was often far beyond the convenience of any road, the isles in which he must sojourn were still partly savage. He must toss much in boats; he must often adventure on horseback by the dubious bridle-track through unfrequented wildernesses; he must sometimes plant his lighthouse in the very camp of wreckers; and he was continually enforced to the vicissitudes of outdoor life. The joy of my grandfather in this career was strong as the love of woman. It lasted him through youth and manhood, it burned strong in age, and at the approach of death his last yearning was to renew these loved experiences. Snared by these interests, the boy seems to have become at once the eager confidant and adviser of his new connection; the Church, if he had ever entertained the prospect very warmly, faded from his view; and at the age of nineteen I find him already in a post of some authority, superintending the construction of the lighthouse on the isle of Little Cumbrae in the Firth of Clyde. The change of aim seems to have caused or been accompanied by a change of character. It sounds absurd to couple the name of my grandfather with the word indolence; but the lad who had been destined from the cradle to the Church, and who had attained the age of fifteen without acquiring more than a moderate knowledge of Latin, was at least no unusual student. From the day of his charge at Little Cumbrae he steps before us what he remained until the end—a man of the most zealous industry, greedy of occupation, greedy of knowledge, a stern husband of time, a reader, a writer, unflagging in his task of self-improvement. Thenceforward his summers were spent directing works and ruling workmen, now in uninhabited, now in half-savage islands; his winters were set apart, first at the Andersonian Institution, then at the University of Edinburgh, to improve himself in mathematics, chemistry, natural history, agriculture, moral philosophy, and logic."

His mother's marriage made a great change also in his domestic life: an only child hitherto, he had become a member of a large family, for his stepfather had already five children. However, "the perilous experiment of bringing together two families for once succeeded. Mr. Smith's two eldest daughters, Jean and Janet, fervent in piety, unwearied in kind deeds, were well qualified both to appreciate and to attract the stepmother," just as her son found immediate favour in the eyes of her husband. Either family, it seems, had been composed of two elements; and in the united household "not only were the women extremely pious, but the men were in reality a trifle worldly. Religious the latter both were; conscious, like all Scots, of the fragility and unreality of that scene in which we play our uncomprehended parts; like all Scots, realising daily and hourly the sense of another will than ours, and a perpetual direction in the affairs of life. But the current of their endeavours flowed in a more obvious channel. They had got on so far, to get on further was their next ambition—to gather wealth, to rise in society, to leave their descendants higher than themselves, to be (in some sense) among the founders of families. Scott was in the same town nourishing similar dreams. But in the eyes of the women these dreams would be foolish and idolatrous."

The connection thus established was destined yet further to affect the life of the young man, and this contrast in the household was still to be perpetuated. "By an extraordinary arrangement, in which it is hard not to suspect the managing hand of a mother, Jean Smith became the wife of Robert Stevenson. The marriage of a man of twenty-seven and a girl of twenty, who have lived for twelve years as brother and sister, is difficult to conceive. It took place, however, and thus in 1799 the family was still further cemented by the union of a representative of the male or worldly element with that of the female and devout.

" This essential difference remained unabridged, yet never diminished the strength of their relation. My grandfather pursued his design of advancing in the world with some measure of success; rose to distinction in his calling, grew to be the familiar of members of Parliament, judges of the Court of Session, and ' landed gentlemen '; learned a ready address, had a flow of interesting conversation, and when he was referred to as ' a highly respectable *bourgeois*,' resented the description. My grandmother remained to the end devout and unambitious, occupied with her Bible, her children, and her house; easily shocked, and associating largely with a clique of godly parasites.

" The cook was a godly woman, the butcher a Christian man, and the table suffered. The scene has been often described to me of my grandfather sawing with darkened countenance at some indissoluble joint—' Preserve me, my dear, what kind of a reedy, stringy beast is this? '—of the joint removed, the pudding substituted and uncovered; and of my grandmother's anxious glance and hasty, deprecatory comment, ' Just mismanaged!' Yet with the invincible obstinacy of soft natures, she would adhere to the godly woman and the Christian man, or find others of the same kidney to replace them."

7

Readers of *Weir of Hermiston* will recognise in this picture the original of Mrs. Weir in all her piety, gentleness, and incompetence, yet in real life " husband and sons all entertained for this pious, tender soul the same chivalrous and moved affection. I have spoken with one who remembered her," her grandson continues, " and who had been the intimate and equal of her sons, and I found this witness had been struck, as I had been, with a sense of disproportion between the warmth of the adoration felt and the nature of the woman, whether as described or observed."

It is no part of my purpose to follow the professional life of Robert Stevenson, which was, moreover, written by his son David. In 1807 he was appointed sole engineer to the Board of Northern Lights, and in the same year began his great work at the Bell Rock, the first lighthouse ever erected far from land upon a reef deeply submerged at every tide.[1] He built twenty lighthouses in all, and introduced many inventions and improvements in the systems of lighting. He did not resign his post until his powers began to fail in 1843, and he died in 1850, four months before the birth of the most famous of his grandsons.

" He began to ail early in that year, and chafed for the period of the annual voyage, which was his medicine and delight. In vain his sons dissuaded him from the adventure. The day approached, the obstinate old gentleman was found in his room, furtively packing a portmanteau, and the truth had to be told him ere he would desist—that he was stricken with a malignant

[1] The Eddystone was scarcely covered at high tide, whereas the Bell Rock was twelve feet below water at such times.

malady, and that before the yacht should have completed her circuit of the lights must himself have started on a more distant cruise. My father has more than once told me of the scene with emotion. The old man was intrepid; he had faced death before with a firm countenance; and I do not suppose he was much dashed at the nearness of our common destiny. But there was something else that would cut him to the quick—the loss of the cruise, the end of all his cruising; the knowledge that he had looked his last on Sumburgh, and the wild crags of Skye, and that Sound of Mull, with the praise of which his letters were so often occupied; that he was never again to hear the surf break in Clashcarnock; never again to see lighthouse after lighthouse (all younger than himself, and the more part of his own device) open in the hour of dusk their flowers of fire, or the topaz and the ruby interchange on the summit of the Bell Rock. To a life of so much activity and danger, a life's work of so much interest and essential beauty, here came a long farewell.[1]

"My grandfather was much of a martinet, and had a habit of expressing himself on paper with an almost startling emphasis. Personally, with his powerful voice, sanguine countenance, and eccentric and original locutions, he was well qualified to inspire a salutary terror in the service. . . . In that service he was king to his finger-tips. All should go in his way, from the principal lightkeeper's coat to the assistant's fender, from the gravel in the garden-walks to the bad smell in the kitchen, or the oil-spots on the storeroom floor. It

[1] " Scott's Voyage in the Lighthouse Yacht," by R. L. S., *Scribner's Magazine*, October, 1893, vol. xiv. p. 493.

might be thought there was nothing more calculated to awake men's resentment, and yet his rule was not more thorough than it was beneficent. His thought for the keepers was continual, and it did not end with their lives. . . . While they lived, he wrote behind their backs to arrange for the education of their children, or to get them other situations if they seemed unsuitable for the Northern Lights. When he was at a lighthouse on a Sunday he held prayers and heard the children read. When a keeper was sick, he lent him his horse and sent him mutton and brandy from the ship. 'The assistant's wife having been this morning confined, there was sent ashore a bottle of sherry and a few rusks —a practice which I have always observed in this service.' . . . No servant of the Northern Lights came to Edinburgh but he was entertained at Baxter's Place to breakfast. There at his own table my grandfather sat down delightedly with his broad-spoken, homespun officers. His whole relation to the service was, in fact, patriarchal; and I believe I may say that throughout its ranks he was adored. I have spoken with many who knew him; I was his grandson, and their words may very well have been words of flattery; but there was one thing that could not be affected, and that was the look and light that came into their faces at the name of Robert Stevenson."

In such a character a love of the picturesque is a trait quite unexpected, and yet in him it existed as a very genuine and active feeling. In the destruction of old buildings and the interference with scenery, inevitable to the engineer, he was careful to secure the best effect and to produce the least possible disfigurement. One road that in the course of his practice he had to design was laid out by him on Hogarth's line of beauty;[1] and of another of his works, the eastern approaches to Edinburgh, Cockburn wrote that "the effect was like drawing up the curtain of a theatre."

Sir Walter Scott accompanied the Commissioners and their officer on one of the annual voyages of the *Pharos* round the coasts of Scotland; his *Journal*, published by Lockhart, shows that he found Robert Stevenson an appreciative and intelligent companion. *The Pirate* and *The Lord of the Isles* were a direct result of this cruise; and it is a curious link in the history of our literature that Scott then visited Skerryvore, the future site of the lighthouse which, as one of the greatest achievements of the Stevenson family, gave its name long afterwards to the only home that their representative in letters ever found in this country.

While the great engineer was the man of action that his grandson longed to be, he also essayed authorship to some purpose. He wrote and published an *Account of the Bell Rock Lighthouse*, which "is of its sort a masterpiece, and has been so recognised by judges; 'the romance of stone and lime,' it has been called, and 'the Robinson Crusoe of engineering,' both happy and descriptive phrases. Even in his letters, though he cannot always be trusted for the construction of his sentences, the same literary virtues are apparent—a strong sense of romance and reality, and an almost infallible instinct for the right detail."[2]

Traits are obliterated and the characteristics of a

[1] Cf. "On Roads," *Juvenilia*, p. 119.
[2] *Scribner's Magazine*, vol. xiv. p. 490.

family may change, but the old man's detestation of everything slovenly or dishonest, "his interest in the whole page of experience, and his perpetual quest and fine scent for all that seems romantic to a boy," were handed down, if ever taste was transmitted, to his grandson. Of the one as of the other it might well have been said that "Perfection was his design." But when we come to Thomas Stevenson, we shall find in him even more of the habits of mind and temper which distinguished his more celebrated son.

Stevenson's mother was the youngest daughter of the Rev. Lewis Balfour, D.D., minister of Colinton, a parish on the stream known as the Water of Leith, five miles to the south-west of Edinburgh. The earliest known member of his family was one Alexander Balfour, placed in charge of the King's Cellar by James IV. in 1499, and of the Queen's Cellar in 1507; he held the lands of Inchrye in Fife, and was in all probability one of the Balfours of Mountquhannie, a numerous family, high in the favour of King James. The descendants of Alexander[1] were chiefly ministers, advocates, or merchants. John Balfour of Kinloch, the Covenanter whom Scott in *Old Mortality* designates Balfour of Burley, may possibly have belonged to this family, but of this there is absolutely no evidence. In the direct line of descent, James Balfour, minister of St. Giles', Edinburgh, from 1589 to 1613, married a niece of Andrew Melville the Reformer, and was, as a brass in his church now records, "one of those who, summoned by

---

[1] His eldest son was David, a name otherwise unknown in the family ; this fact was only re-discovered several years after the publication of *Kidnapped*. So does reality supplement fiction.

James VI. to Hampton Court in 1606, refused to sur-
render their principles to his desires for the establishment of Episcopacy in Scotland." James, born 1680,
whose father was one of the Governors of the Darien
Company, bought the estate of Pilrig, lying between
Edinburgh and Leith, with which the family has ever
since been connected, and to which David Balfour is
brought in *Catriona*. The laird whom David met was
James, born 1705, who, having studied at Leyden, became Professor of Moral Philosophy in the University
of Edinburgh, and then exchanged this Chair for that
of the Laws of Nature and Nations. His wife was a
daughter of Sir John Elphinstone of Logie and granddaughter of Sir Gilbert Elliot, known as Lord Minto, a
judge of the Court of Session. It was through this
connection that Stevenson was able to say, " I have
shaken a spear in the Debatable Land and shouted the
slogan of the Elliots." The Professor's son, John Balfour, father of the minister of Colinton, married his
cousin Jean Whyte; and so by this marriage Stevenson's
mother was a second cousin of the novelist, Major
George Whyte-Melville.

Lewis Balfour was born at Pilrig in 1777; about the
age of twenty he showed symptoms of a weak chest,
and was sent for a winter to the Isle of Wight with the
most entire success. On returning, he took orders,
went to his first Ayrshire parish, and there fell in love
with and married a daughter of Dr. Smith of Galston,
the Dr. Smith who in Burns's *Holy Fair* " opens out his
cauld harangues on practice and on morals." In 1823
he came to the parish of Colinton, and there remained
until his death thirty-seven years later. In 1844 he lost

his wife, a woman of great personal beauty and sweetness of character, and the management of the household fell into the hands of his eldest unmarried daughter. His is the manse of *Memories and Portraits*, the favourite home of his grandson's childhood. The essay in question describes him " as a man of singular simplicity of nature; unemotional, and hating the display of what he felt; standing contented on the old ways; a lover of his life and innocent habits to the end. We children admired him—partly for his beautiful face and silver hair, for none more than children are concerned for beauty, and, above all, for beauty in the old; partly for the solemn light in which we beheld him once a week, the observed of all observers, in the pulpit. But his strictness and distance, the effect, I now fancy, of old age, slow blood, and settled habit, oppressed us with a kind of terror. . . . He had no idea of spoiling children, leaving all that to my aunt; he had fared hard himself, and blubbered under the rod in the last century; and his ways were still Spartan for the young. . . . When not abroad, he sat much alone, writing sermons or letters to his scattered family in a dark and cold room with a library of bloodless books—and these lonely hours wrapped him in the greater gloom for our imaginations. But the study had a redeeming grace in many Indian pictures, gaudily coloured and dear to young eyes. I cannot depict (for I have no such passions now) the greed with which I beheld them; and when I was once sent in to say a psalm to my grandfather, I went, quaking indeed with fear, but at the same time glowing with hope that if I said it well, he might reward me with an Indian picture.

14

' Thy foot He 'll not let slide, nor will
He slumber that thee keeps,'

it ran—a strange conglomerate of the unpronounce-
able, a sad model to set in childhood before one who
was himself to be a versifier, and a task in recitation
that really merited reward.

" And I must suppose the old man thought so too, and
was either touched or amused by the performance; for
he took me in his arms with most unwonted tenderness
and kissed me, and gave me a little kindly sermon for
my psalm; so that, for that day, we were clerk and
parson." The picture was not given (how should it
have been?) but on that, and more than one other occasion, the minister showed himself in a very kind and
sympathetic mood to his little kinsman. "Try as I
please," wrote the grandson in later days, "I cannot
join myself on with the reverend doctor; and all the
while, no doubt, and even as I write the phrase, he
moves in my blood, and whispers words to me, and
sits efficient in the very knot and centre of my being."
Yet even if no individual traits or physical resem-
blances can be traced to the old minister, much of the
general Scottish cast of character in Stevenson—the
"strong Scots accent of the mind"—was confirmed by
this strain; and it is evident that his intensity, his ethical preoccupations, and, as he himself says, his "love
of preaching" were due, at all events in part, to the
fact that he was a " grandson of the manse."

Such, at any rate, was the history of his maternal
ancestors, the Balfours, a family who possessed in a
high degree the domestic virtues of the Lowland Scot.

The laird of Pilrig in *Catriona*, who was drawn (as far as possible) from existing records, was no unfair representative of them all: when good or evil, honour or dishonour, were presented to them as alternatives, there would be no hesitation in their choice, but they were rarely surprised in so distressing a dilemma. Till after the date I have reached, few of the cadets ever sought their fortunes abroad, though the next generation was more enterprising, and four out of Mrs. Stevenson's five brothers spent much of their lives in India or New Zealand. But for the most part the family were stay-at-home folk, and adventures, which are to the adventurous, came not near their peaceful dwellings.

From Stevensons, Balfours, and the two families of Smiths, their descendant turned to see if he could find no trace of any origin more stimulating or more romantic. The name of Stevenson seemed to him Norse; or again, he clung to a very vague tradition that his father's family was "somehow descended from a French barber surgeon who came to St. Andrews in the service of one of the Cardinal Beatons."

Even more fascinating was the theory based on nothing more than the fact that Stevenson was used permanently as a surname by some of the proscribed Macgregors. To have proved himself a disguised clansman of Rob Roy, and to have had James Mohr for the black sheep of the family, was a dream which it was worth a world of pains to verify; and the possibility that James Stevenson in Glasgow "may have had a Highland *alias* upon his conscience and a claymore in his back parlour" was too delightful to be let go without a struggle. But death interrupted these inquiries, and for these shadowy speculations there seems to be no ground in history. Mr. J. H. Stevenson of Edinburgh, a namesake, and a specialist in these matters, has investigated the question dispassionately and thoroughly, and his conclusion[1] is that all theories of a possible Norse, Highland, or French origin are vain; that this family can be traced only to the stock of Westland Whigs settled in the end of the seventeenth century in the parish of Neilston; and that it is impossible to say anything about the date or origin of their first settlement in the locality. The most striking fact about them as a whole is, after all, the contrast between "this undistinguished perpetuation of a family throughout the centuries, and the sudden bursting forth of character and capacity" that began with Robert Stevenson.

If it be difficult to follow his ancestors, it is manifestly impossible to find any safe ground for speculating on the race to which Stevenson belonged. None of his forbears for many centuries, so far as we can tell, were newcomers to Scotland; and it is probable that in him, as in almost any other native of the same region, several strains of the long-established races were combined. The word "Balfour," as Cluny reminds us in *Kidnapped*, is "good Gaelic," its meaning being "cold croft or farm." The place of that name is in Fife. The estate was held by the Bethunes for five hundred years, until recently it passed again into the hands of a Balfour "of that ilk." But the appellation of a family need signify no more than the former possession of some holding to which the Celts had already given a name, and the Balfours of Pilrig belonged apparently to an

[1] *Family of Engineers*, p. 201, note.

17

East Lowland type. Renfrew, on the other hand, was part of the Celtic kingdom of the Britons of Alclyde, and it was in that territory that the name of Stevenson has been chiefly found, and that this particular family was settled. Neither name nor locality, however, is any sure guide to an origin so remote; and we can be certain of no more than this, that Louis Stevenson and his father and grandfather exhibited many moods and tendencies of mind attributed to the Celtic race.

CHAPTER II

HIS PARENTS

" We are the pledge of their dear and joyful union, we have been the solicitude of their days and the anxiety of their nights, we have made them, though by no will of ours, to carry the burden of our sins, sorrows, and physical infirmities. . . . A good son, who can fulfil what is expected of him, has done his work in life. He has to redeem the sins of many, and restore the world's confidence in children."—R. L. S., " Reflections and Remarks on Human Life," *Miscellanea*, p. 27.

" Peace and her huge invasion to these shores
  Puts daily home; innumerable sails
  Dawn on the far horizon and draw near;
  Innumerable loves, uncounted hopes
  To our wild coasts, not darkling now, approach:
  Not now obscure, since thou and thine are there,
  And bright on the lone isle, the foundered reef,
  The long, resounding foreland, Pharos stands.
  These are thy works, O father, these thy crown."
    R. L. S., *Underwoods*, xxviii.

WITHOUT a knowledge of his parents it would be hard to understand the man whose life and character are set forth in these pages.   Yet of Thomas Stevenson, at any rate, I should despair of presenting any adequate image, were it not for the sketch in *Memories and Portraits*, and an account of his boyhood, written by his son in 1887, and as yet unpublished, which would have formed a later chapter of *A Family of Engineers*.

He was born in 1818, the youngest son of Robert Stevenson, and one of a family of thirteen children.

"He had his education at a private school, kept by a capable but very cruel man called Brown, in Nelson Street, and then at the High School of Edinburgh. His first year, or half-year, was in the old building down Infirmary Street, and I have often heard him tell how he took part in the procession to the new and beautiful place upon the Calton Hill. Piper was his master, a fellow much given to thrashing. He never seems to have worked for any class that he attended; and in Piper's took a place about half-way between the first and last of a hundred and eighty boys. Yet his friends were among the duxes. He tells most admirably how he once on a chance question got to the top of the class among all his friends; and how they kept him there for several days by liberal prompting and other obvious devices, until at last he himself wearied of the fierce light that beat upon the upper benches. 'It won't do,' he said. 'Good-bye.' And being left to his own resources, he rapidly declined, and before that day was over was half-way back again to his appropriate level. It is an odd illustration of how carelessly a class was then taught in spite of the many stripes. I remember how my own Academy master, the delightful D'Arcy Thompson, not forty years later, smelling a capable boy among the boobies, persecuted the bottom of the class for four days, with the tawse going at a great rate; until the event amply justified his suspicion, and an inveterate booby, M—— by name, shot up some forty places, and was ever afterwards a decent, if not a distinguished pupil.

"On one occasion my father absented himself from the idle shows of the Exhibition day, and went off rambling to Portobello. His father attributed this escapade to social cowardice because of his humble position in the class. It was what in his picturesque personal dialect the old man called 'Turkeying'; he made my father's life a burthen to him in consequence; and long after (months, I think—certainly weeks) my grandfather, who was off upon his tour of inspection, wrote home to Baxter's Place in one of his emphatic, inimitable letters: 'The memory of Tom's weakness haunts me like a ghost.' My father looked for this in vain among the letter-books not long ago; but the phrase is expressly autochthonic; it had been burned into his memory by the disgrace of the moment when it was read aloud at the breakfast-table.

"At least it shows, at once and finally, the difference between father and son. Robert took education and success at school for a thing of infinite import; to Thomas, in his young independence, it all seemed Vanity of Vanities. He would not have been ashamed to figure as actual booby before His Majesty the King. Indeed, there seems to have been nothing more rooted in him than his contempt for all the ends, processes, and ministers of education. Tutor was ever a by-word with him; 'positively tutorial,' he would say of people or manners he despised; and with rare consistency, he bravely encouraged me to neglect my lessons, and never so much as asked me my place in school. . . .

"My father's life, in the meantime, and the truly formative parts of his education, lay entirely in his hours of play. I conceive him as a very sturdy and madly high-spirited boy. Early one Saturday, gambolling and tricksying about the kitchen, it occurred to him to use

Cayenne pepper as snuff; no sooner said than done; and the rest of that invaluable holiday was passed, as you may fancy, with his nose under the kitchen spout.

"No. 1 Baxter's Place, my grandfather's house, must have been a paradise for boys. It was of great size, with an infinity of cellars below, and of garrets, apple-lofts, etc., above; and it had a long garden, which ran down to the foot of the Calton Hill, with an orchard that yearly filled the apple-loft, and a building at the foot frequently besieged and defended by the boys, where a poor golden eagle, trophy of some of my grandfather's Hebridean voyages, pined and screamed itself to death. Its front was Leith Walk with its traffic; at one side a very deserted lane, with the office door, a carpenter's shop, and the like; and behind, the big, open slopes of the Calton Hill. Within, there was the seemingly rather awful rule of the old gentleman, tempered, I fancy, by the mild and devout mother with her 'Keep me's.' There was a coming and going of odd, out-of-the-way characters, skippers, lightkeepers, masons, and foremen of all sorts, whom my grand-father, in his patriarchal fashion, liked to have about the house, and who were a never-failing delight to the boys. Tutors shed a gloom for an hour or so in the evening . . . and these and that accursed school-going were the black parts of their life. But there were, every Saturday, extraordinary doings in Baxter's Place. Willie Swan, my father's first cousin, and chief friend from boyhood, since Professor of Natural Philosophy at St. Andrews, would be there; and along with him a tribe of other cousins. All these boys together had great times, as you may fancy. There were cellars full of barrels, of which they made fortifications; sometimes on the stair, at a great risk to life and limb. There was the eagle-house in the garden, often held and assaulted as a fort. Once my father, finding a piece of iron chimney-pot—an 'auld wife,' as we say in Scotland—brought it home and donned it as a helmet in the next Saturday's wars. I doubt if he ever recovered from his disappointment over the result; for the helmet, far from rendering him an invulnerable champion, an Achilles of the field, turned him into a mere blind and helpless popinjay, spurned and hustled by every one; and, as well as I remember the story, he was at last ignominiously captured by the other side.

" They were all, I gather, quaint boys, and had quaint enjoyments. One diversion of theirs was to make up little parcels of ashes, labelled ' Gold Dust, with care, to Messrs. Marshall & Co., Jewellers,' or whatever the name might be, leave them lying in a quiet street, and conceal themselves hard by to follow the result. If an honest man came by, he would pick it up, read the superscription, and march off with it towards Marshall's, nothing fearing; though God knows what his reception may have been. This was not their quarry. But now and again there would come some slippery being, who glanced swiftly and guiltily up and down the street, and then, with true legerdemain, whipped the thing into his pocket. Such an one would be closely dogged, and not for long either; his booty itched in his pocket; he would dodge into the first common-stair, whence there might come, as my father used to say, ' a blaff of ashes '; and a human being, justly indignant at the imposition, would stalk forth out of the common-stair and go his way.

" Every summer the family went to Portobello. The Portobello road is rather a dreary one to ordinary mortals, but to my father it was, I believe, the most romantic four miles of all Christendom; he had looked at it so often from the carriage-windows during the annual family removal, his heart beating high for the holidays; he had walked it so often to go bathing; he knew so many stories and had so rich a treasure of association about every corner of the way. . . . He had a collection of curiosities, like so many other boys, his son included; he had a printing-press, and printed some sort of dismal paper on the *Spectator* plan, which did not, I think, ever get over the first page. He had a chest of chemicals, and made all manner of experiments, more or less abortive, as boys' experiments will be. But there was always a remarkable inconsequence, an unconscious spice of the true Satanic, rebel nature, in the boy. Whatever he played with was the reverse of what he was formally supposed to be engaged in learning. As soon as he went, for instance, to a class of chemistry, there were no more experiments made by him. The thing then ceased to be a pleasure, and became an irking drudgery."

Robert Stevenson had intended only one of his sons to follow his own profession. But in the end their natural tastes prevailed, and no less than three of the brothers entered the business, practised it at large with great ability and success, and were all three, conjointly or in turn, appointed to the official post their father and grandfather had held of engineer to the Board of Northern Lights. Thomas Stevenson did much valuable work in lighthouse building and in the improvement of rivers and harbours, but it is in connection with the illumination of lighthouses that his name will be remembered. He brought to perfection the revolving light, and himself invented "the azimuthal condensing system." More familiar to the world at large, if less remarkable, are the louvre-boarded screens which he applied to the protection of meteorological instruments. He became, moreover, a recognised authority on engineering; he gave much weighty evidence before Parliamentary committees; and his position in the scientific world was marked in 1884 by his election to the Presidentship of the Royal Society of Edinburgh.

His entire life was devoted to the unremitting pursuit of a scientific profession, in which it was his dearest wish to see his son following in his footsteps; yet it was from him that Louis derived all the romantic and artistic elements that drew him away from engineering, and were the chief means by which he became an acknowledged master of his art.

The apparent inconsistencies of the father were numerous, but all of them were such as add force and picturesqueness to a character, and only increased the affection of those who knew and understood him most thoroughly.

"He was a man," writes his son,[1] "of a somewhat antique strain; with a blended sternness and softness that was wholly Scottish and at first somewhat bewildering; with a profound essential melancholy of disposition and (what often accompanies it) the most humorous geniality in company; shrewd and childish; passionately attached, passionately prejudiced; a man

[1] *Memories and Portraits*, p. 175.

of many extremes, many faults of temper, and no very stable foothold for himself among life's troubles. Yet he was a wise adviser; many men, and these not inconsiderable, took counsel with him habitually. . . . He had excellent taste, though whimsical and partial; . . . took a lasting pleasure in prints and pictures; . . . and, though he read little, was constant to his favourite books. He had never any Greek; Latin he happily retaught himself after he had left school, where he was a mere consistent idler; happily, I say, for Lactantius, Vossius, and Cardinal Bona were his chief authors. The first he must have read for twenty years uninterruptedly, keeping it near him in his study, and carrying it in his bag on journeys. Another old theologian, Brown of Wamphray, was often in his hands. When he was indisposed, he had two books, *Guy Mannering* and *The Parent's Assistant*,[1] of which he never wearied. He was a strong Conservative or, as he preferred to call himself, a Tory; except in so far as his views were modified by a hot-headed chivalrous sentiment for women. He was actually in favour of a marriage law under which any woman might have a divorce for the asking, and no man on any ground whatever; and the same sentiment found another expression in a Magdalen Mission in Edinburgh, founded and largely supported by himself. This was but one of the many channels of his public generosity; his private was equally unrestrained. The Church of Scotland, of which he held the doctrines (though in a sense of his own), and to which he bore a clansman's loyalty, profited often by his time and

[1] His copy of Miss Edgeworth's book is filled with the most entertaining notes.

26

money; and though, from a morbid sense of his own unworthiness, he would never consent to be an office-bearer, his advice was often sought, and he served the Church on many committees. What he perhaps valued highest in his work were his contributions to the defence of Christianity; one of which, in particular, was praised by Hutchison Stirling, and reprinted at the request of Professor Crawford.

"His sense of his own unworthiness I have called morbid; morbid, too, were his sense of the fleetingness of life and his concern for death. He had never accepted the conditions of man's life or his own character; and his inmost thoughts were ever tinged with the Celtic melancholy. Cases of conscience were sometimes grievous to him, and that delicate employment of a scientific witness cost him many qualms. But he found respite from these troublesome humours in his work, in his lifelong study of natural science, in the society of those he loved, and in his daily walks, which now would carry him far into the country with some congenial friend, and now keep him dangling about the town from one old book-shop to another, and scraping romantic acquaintance with every dog that passed. His talk, compounded of so much sterling sense and so much freakish humour, and clothed in language so apt, droll, and emphatic, was a perpetual delight to all who knew him before the clouds began to settle on his mind. His use of language was both just and picturesque; and when at the beginning of his illness he began to feel the ebbing of this power, it was strange and painful to hear him reject one word after another as inadequate, and at length desist from the search and leave his phrase unfinished rather than finish it without propriety. It was perhaps another Celtic trait that his affections and emotions, passionate as these were and liable to passionate ups and downs, found the most eloquent expression both in words and gestures. Love, anger, and indignation shone through him and broke forth in imagery, like what we read of Southern races. For all these emotional extremes, and in spite of the melancholy ground of his character, he had upon the whole a happy life; nor was he less fortunate in his death, which at the last came to him unaware."

The characteristics of the father in his boyhood might be ascribed with little alteration to his son. The circumstances differed, but the spirit, the freaks, and the idleness were the same. To increase the truth or to add to the beauty of the later picture is almost beyond the power of any one, but in the present connection it may be permissible to dwell a little upon the romantic side of Thomas Stevenson. Every night of his life he made up stories by which he put himself to sleep, dealing perpetually "with ships, roadside inns, robbers, old sailors, and commercial travellers before the era of steam." With these and their like he soothed his son's troubled nights in childhood, and when the son grew up and made stories of his own, he found no critic more unsparing than his father, and none more ready to take fire at "*his* own kind of picturesque." Many were the changes adopted on his proposal; and his suggestions extended to words and style as well as matter. "Mercy on us!" he wrote in 1885, "your story should always be as plain as plumb porridge." He was fanatical in the heresy that art should invariably have a conscious

28

moral aim, but except in this his judgments were serviceable and shrewd.

The differences between the pair were slight, the points of resemblance many. The younger man devoted his life to art and not to science, and the hold of dogma upon him was early relaxed. But the humour and the melancholy, the sternness and the softness, the attachments and the prejudices, the chivalry, the generosity, the Celtic temperament, and the sensitive conscience passed direct from father to son in proportions but slightly varied, and to some who knew them both well the father was the more remarkable of the two. One period of misunderstanding they had, but it was brief, and might have been avoided had either of the pair been less sincere or less in earnest. Afterwards, and perhaps as a consequence, their comprehension and appreciation of each other grew complete, and their attachment was even deeper than that usually subsisting between father and only son. In the conditions of their lives there was this further difference: if the son missed the healthy boyhood, full of games and of companions, he was spared at the last the failure which he also dreaded; no less fortunate than his father in the unconsciousness of his death, he died before his prime and the fulness of his power, "in mid-career laying out vast projects," and so "trailing with him clouds of glory," he was taken away as one whom the gods loved.

Of Mrs. Thomas Stevenson not a line of any sketch remains among the work of her son: a want easily explained by the fact that she survived him. It is the more necessary to supply in some measure this deficiency, as the warmth of Louis' gratitude to his nurse has unjustly reacted to the prejudice of his mother, and has quite wrongly been supposed by those who did not know them to indicate neglect on one side and on the other a lack of affection.

In person she was tall, slender, and graceful; and her face and fair complexion retained their beauty, as her figure and walk preserved their elasticity, to the last. Her vivacity and brightness were most attractive; she made on strangers a quick and lasting impression, and the letters written on the news of her death attest the devotion and number of her friends. As a hostess she had great social tact, and her hospitality was but the expression of her true kindliness of heart.

Her undaunted spirit led her when nearly sixty to accompany her son, first to America, and then, in a racing schooner, through the remotest groups of the Pacific, finally to settle with him in the disturbed spot where he had chosen his home.

She had in the highest degree that readiness for en-joyment which makes light of discomfort, and turns into a holiday any break of settled routine. Her desire to be pleased, her prompt interest in any experience, however new or unexpected, her resolute refusal to see the unpleasant side of things, all had their counterpart in her son, enabling him to pass through the many dark hours, that would have borne far more heavily upon his father's temperament.

Frail though his own constitution was, his early visits to various health-resorts were due in the first instance to the need of securing a better climate for his mother, who unfortunately fell into ill-health during the ten or twelve years of his boyhood. When he was ailing, she was often ill at the same time, and was frequently disabled from performing for him the services it would have been her greatest delight to render.

But of her devotion and of her incessant thought for the boy there can be no question. I have before me as I write a series of pocket-diaries, complete (but for the second year) from 1851 until the year of her death. The earlier books are occupied exclusively with her husband and her child, and in the later volumes these two are still the staple of her entries. Louis' place in class is scrupulously noted, and that, we may be sure, with no encouragement from his father. When he was small, she read to him a great deal, and to her he owed his first acquaintance with much that is best in literature. Almost every scrap of his writing that ever passed into her hands was treasured. His first efforts at tales or histories, taken down by herself, or some other amanuensis, before he was able or willing to write; nearly every letter he ever sent her; every compliment to him, and every word of praise — all were carefully preserved, long before he showed any definite promise of becoming famous; and by her method and accuracy she was able to record for his biographer, with hardly an exception, where he spent each month of his life. The story of almost the only letter she did not keep bears so directly on her character that I must set it down in her words. "In the spring of 1872 Louis was in a very depressed state; he wrote one terribly morbid letter to me from Dunblane, all about death and churchyards — it vexed me so much that I put it in the fire at once. Years after, when he was writing his

31

essay 'Old Mortality,' he applied to me for that letter, and was quite vexed when I told him that I had destroyed it."

The son's attachment to his mother was no less deep and lasting. The earliest record of it goes back to his very infancy, when, at three years old, he was left alone with her one day in the dining-room after dinner. He had seen his nurse cover her mistress with a shawl at such times; so he took a doyley off the table, unfolded it, and carefully spread it over her, saying, "That's a wee bittie, mama." Another speech of his two years later was, "I'm going to call you 'Mother' sometimes, just that I may remember to do it when I'm a big man." And he ended the same day with "Goodnight, my jewelest of mothers." This loving attention to her continued during his whole life. Through all her illnesses and whenever she needed his care, he was always most sedulous and affectionate, displaying at times a tenderness almost feminine. The most irregular of correspondents, he was almost regular to her; master of his pen though he was, several times after he had become a man of letters he bursts out into impatience at the difficulty he finds in expressing to her and to his father the depth of his affection and gratitude to them both. He kept numbers of her letters, even of those received during the most migratory periods of his life; and soon after his marriage, though his wife was the most devoted and capable of nurses, on the outbreak of an illness, like a child he turned to his mother and would be satisfied with nothing short of her presence.

After his father's death, when the doctors had ordered

him to go to America, if he wanted to live, he wrote to her: "Not only would we not go to America without you; we should not persist in trying it, if we did not believe that it would be on the whole the best for you." From that time, but for two absences in Scotland, she made her home with him and his family, and had the reward of realising that the exile which severed him from so many of his friends had brought her to an even more intimate knowledge of his life and an even closer place in his affection.

CHAPTER III

"I please myself often by saying that I had a Covenanting child-hood."— R. L. S., MS. fragment.

"I am one of the few people in the world who do not forget their own lives."— R. L. S., *Letters*, ii. 107.

ROBERT LEWIS BALFOUR STEVENSON was born at No. 8 Howard Place, Edinburgh, on the 13th November, 1850, and a few days after his birth was baptized by his grandfather, the minister of Colinton, according to the Scots custom, in his father's house. He was called after his two grandfathers, and to their names that of his mother's family was added.[1]

---

[1] It was as Robert Louis Stevenson that he was known to all the world, and the earlier variations of his name, remembered but by few, are of small importance. Nevertheless it may be as well to set them down here.

In his earliest letters, and down to 1865, the boy signed himself " R. Stevenson." After that he occasionally used " R. L. B. Stevenson," but in 1868 asked his mother in place of this to address him as " Robert Lewis." For the next five years he was generally but not invariably " R. L. Stevenson," until about 1873 the final change is marked by his usage and an undated letter to Mr. Baxter belonging to this period (now the property of the Savile Club). " After several years of feeble and ineffectual endeavour with regard to my third initial (a thing I loathe), I have been led to put myself out of reach of such accident in the future by taking my first two names in full."

The Pentland Rising was published in 1866, without the author's name; the first magazine article, " On Roads," in the *Portfolio* for December, 1873, was signed " L. S. Stoneven," and *Treasure Island* and *The Black Arrow* appeared in *Young Folks* as " by Captain

His birthplace was the home which Thomas Stevenson had prepared for his bride two years before; a
small, unpretentious, comfortable stone house, forming
part of a row still standing, situated on low ground
just to the north of the Water of Leith. Two and a
half years later this was changed for No. 1 Inverleith
Terrace, a more commodious dwelling on the other
side of the same road; but that, having three outside
walls, proved too cold for the delicate boy. Accordingly, in 1857, the little family of three—for Louis remained an only child—moved half a mile further south
into what was then the centre of the New Town, and

George North." With these exceptions, all his work, but the very
small part of it which was anonymous, was formally announced as
by "Robert Louis Stevenson," or, in the case of the *Cornhill Magazine*, by "R. L. S."; initials, says Mr. Barrie, "the best beloved in
recent literature "

The change of the name of Lewis from the Scots form to the French
was made when he was about eighteen; the exact date is not easy to
fix on account of his practice of using the initial only in his signature
at that period. The alteration was due, it is said, to a strong distaste,
shared by his father, for a fellow-citizen, who bore the name in the
form in which Lewis had received it. But it was only the spelling
that Stevenson changed and never the pronunciation. Lewis he remained at all times in the mouth of his family and of his intimate
friends.

From his infancy his father called him "Smout" or "Smoutie"
(*i.e.* smolt, young salmon, small fry), and this continued to be his pet
name through childhood. When he was in his tenth year, his mother
changes finally to "Lou" in her diary; but the early name was only
abolished several years later by means of the fine of a penny, which
the boy exacted for each offence from every one who employed it.

"Robert," says his mother, "was his school name, but it was never
used at home," one reason perhaps being that his cousin, R. A. M.
Stevenson, was already known in the family as "Bob."

occupied No. 17 Heriot Row, which continued to be their home in Edinburgh for thirty years. This was a substantial house of grey stone, built with the solidity so customary in Scotland and so unusual in the South, looking across the Queen Street Gardens, where the lilacs bloomed in spring and the pipe of the blackbird might be heard; while from its back windows could be seen the hills of "the kingdom of Fife."

For the first year of his life the infant seemed healthy and made satisfactory progress. He climbed a stair of eighteen steps at nine months, at eleven months walked freely, and in two months more called people by their names. But with his mother's brightness of disposition he had unfortunately inherited also from her a weakness of chest and a susceptibility to cold, which affected the whole course of his life. When he was a little over two he had a severe attack of croup, and from that time until he was eleven there was no year in which he was not many days in bed from illness—bronchitis, pneumonia, feverish cold, or chills affecting his digestion, as well as one severe gastric fever, and all the ordinary maladies of childhood in rapid succession. In the summer months he kept fairly well, and was then for most of his time away from Edinburgh at Portobello, Lasswade, Bridge of Allan, Burntisland, North Berwick, Aberdour, or some other of the Edinburgh summer resorts as yet frequented by few visitors. It was to the manse at Colinton, however, that he most frequently went until the death of his grandfather in 1860, and it was here, as we shall see, that the happiest days of his childhood were passed.

Of his earliest memories he speaks thus:—

36

"I remember with particular pleasure running up-stairs in Inverleith Terrace with my mother — herself little more than a girl — to the top flat of this our second house, both of us singing as best we could "We'll all go up to Gatty's room, to Gatty's room, etc.," *ad lib.*; Gatty being contracted for Grandpapa, my mother's father, who was coming to stay with us. I mention that because it stands out in stronger relief than any other recollection of the same age. I have a great belief in these vivid recollections: things that impress us so forcibly as to become stereotyped for life have not done so for nothing.

"I believe I was what is called a good child: I learned large passages of Scripture and hymns, and recited them, I understand, with very good action and emphasis. After I was in bed I used to be heard lying awake and repeating to myself — crooning over to myself in the dark — certain curious rambling effusions, which I called my 'songstries.' One of these, which was taken down by my father, who stood outside the door for the purpose, I have seen; it was in a sort of rhythmic prose, curiously approximating to ten-syllable blank verse, and was religious in its bearing; I think it is now lost." [1]

The following appears to be the songstry in question: [2] it is dated April 23rd, 1857: —

"Had not an angel got the pride of man,
No evil thought, no hardened heart would have been
    seen.

[1] Unpublished MS., dated 18th May, 1873.
[2] There is a singular parallel at an even earlier age in the *Life of Charles Kingsley.*

No hell to go to, but a heaven so pure;
That angel was the Devil.
Had not that angel got the pride, there would have
    been no need
For Jesus Christ to die upon the cross."

"That I was eminently religious, there can be no
doubt. I had an extreme terror of Hell, implanted in
me, I suppose, by my good nurse, which used to haunt
me terribly on stormy nights, when the wind had
broken loose and was going about the town like a bed-
lamite. I remember that the noises on such occasions
always grouped themselves for me into the sound of a
horseman, or rather a succession of horsemen, riding
furiously past the bottom of the street and away up the
hill into town; I think even now that I hear the terrible
howl of his passage, and the clinking that I used to
attribute to his bit and stirrups. On such nights I
would lie awake and pray and cry, until I prayed and
cried myself asleep; and if I can form any notion of
what an earnest prayer should be, I imagine that mine
were such.[1] . . .

"All this time, be it borne in mind, my health was of
the most precarious description. Many winters I never
crossed the threshold; but used to lie on my face on
the nursery floor, chalking or painting in water-colours
the pictures in the illustrated newspapers; or sit up in
bed, with a little shawl pinned about my shoulders, to
play with bricks or whatnot. I remember the pleasant
maternal casuistry by which I was allowed to retain
my playthings of a Sunday, when a pack was sewn

---

[1] Cf. " Nuits Blanches," *Juvenilia*, p. 35.

on to the back of one of the wooden figures, and I had then duly promised to play at nothing but 'Pilgrim's Progress.' . . . Although I was never done drawing and painting, and even kept on doing so until I was seventeen or eighteen, I never had any real pictorial vision, and instead of trying to represent what I saw, was merely imitating the general appearance of other people's representations. I never drew a picture of anything that was before me, but always from fancy, a sure sign of the absence of artistic eyesight; and I beautifully illustrated my lack of real feeling for art, by a very early speech, which I have had repeated to me by my mother: 'Mama,' said I, 'I have drawed a man. Shall I draw his soul now?'

" My ill-health principally chronicles itself by the terrible long nights that I lay awake, troubled continually with a hacking, exhausting cough, and praying for sleep or morning from the bottom of my shaken little body. I principally connect these nights, however, with our third house, in Heriot Row; and cannot mention them without a grateful testimony to the unwearied sympathy and long-suffering displayed to me on a hundred such occasions by my good nurse. It seems to me that I should have died if I had been left there alone to cough and weary in the darkness. How well I remember her lifting me out of bed, carrying me to the window, and showing me one or two lit windows up in Queen Street across the dark belt of gardens; where also, we told each other, there might be sick little boys and their nurses waiting, like us, for the morning.[1] Other night scenes connected with my ill-health were

1 Cf. *Underwoods*, No. xxvi., " The Sick Child."

the little sallies of delirium that used to waken me out
of a feverish sleep, in such agony of terror as, thank
God, I have never suffered since.[1]   My father had generally to come up and sit by my bedside, and feign
conversations with guards or coachmen or innkeepers,
until I was gradually quieted and brought to myself;
but it was long after one of those paroxysms before I
could bear to be left alone."

When Louis was a little child, he accidentally locked
himself into a room alone one day.   He could not turn
the key again as he was directed; darkness was coming
on, and his terror became extreme.   His father sent for
a locksmith to open the door, and during the period of
waiting talked to Louis through the keyhole, the child
becoming so engrossed by the charm of his father's
conversation that he forgot all his fears.

His nurse was, it will already be seen, even more
than is usual with children, an important factor in his
life.   When he was eighteen months old, Alison Cunningham — " Cummie " to him for the rest of his days

[1] One of the causes of his panic " seems to indicate," as he says, " a
considerable force of imagination.   I dreamed I was to swallow the
world, and the terror of the fancy arose from the complete conception
I had of the hugeness and populousness of our sphere.   Disproportion
and a peculiar shade of brown, something like that of sealskin, haunted
me particularly during these visitations."   For a further description of
these early dreams the reader may refer to *Additional Memories and
Portraits*, p. 318.   To the sense of disproportion may be ascribed the
version for the *Child's Garden*, xxiv.:

" The world is so great and I am so small,
I do not like it at all, at all,"

which afterwards passed into the well-known brave and characteristic
" Happy Thought."

— came to him and watched over his childhood with the most intense devotion. She refused, it is said, an offer of marriage, that she might not have to leave her charge, and she remained with the family long after the care of him had passed out of women's hands, never taking another place, as indeed she had no need to do. Her true reward has been a monument of gratitude for which a parallel is hard to find. At twenty (an age when young men are not generally very tender to such memories) Louis wrote the paper on Nurses printed in *Juvenilia*. Fifteen years later the dedication of the *Child's Garden* was "To Alison Cunningham, From Her Boy," and this was but the preface to one of the happiest sets of verses in one of the happiest of books. Alison Hastie, the lass at Limekilns, who put David Balfour and Alan Breck across the Forth, was, he told her, an ancestress of hers, just as David was a kinsman of his own. Of all his works he sent her copies; throughout his life he wrote letters to her; when he had a house, he had her to stay with him, and even proposed to bring her out on a visit to Samoa. In another fragment of autobiography he has again described her services: "My recollections of the long nights when I was kept awake by coughing are only relieved by the thought of the tenderness of my nurse and second mother (for my first will not be jealous), Alison Cunningham. She was more patient than I can suppose of an angel; hours together she would help and console me . . . till the whole sorrow of the night was at an end with the arrival of the first of that long string of country carts, that in the dark hours of the morning, with the neighing of horses, the cracking of

In matters of conduct Cummie was for no half-measures. Cards were the Devil's books. Mr. and Mrs. Stevenson played whist, decorous family whist — the mother had the keenest zest for all games — and Louis could remember praying fervently with his nurse that it might not be visited on them to their perdition. The novel and the playhouse were alike anathema to her; and this would seem no very likely opening for the career of one who was to be a novelist and write plays as well. For her pupil entered fully into the spirit of her ordinances, and insisted on a most rigorous observance of her code.

"I was brought up on *Cassell's Family Paper*," he wrote, "but the lady who was kind enough to read the tales aloud to me was subject to sharp attacks of conscience. She took the *Family Paper* on confidence; the tales it contained being Family Tales, not novels. But every now and then, something would occur to alarm her finer sense; she would express a well-grounded fear that the current fiction was 'going to turn out a regular novel,' and the *Family Paper*, with my pious approval, would be dropped. Yet neither she nor I were wholly stoical; and when Saturday came round, we would study the windows of the stationer, and try to fish out of subsequent woodcuts and their legends the further adventures of our favourites." [1]

In spite of her restrictions, Cummie was full of life and merriment. She danced and sang to her boy, and read to him most dramatically. She herself tells how, the last time she ever saw him, he said to her, "before a room full of people, 'It's *you* that gave me a passion for the drama, Cummie.' 'Me, Master Lou,'

[1] *Scribner's Magazine*, July, 1888.

I said; 'I never put foot inside a playhouse in my life.' 'Ay, woman,' said he; 'but it was the grand dramatic way ye had of reciting the hymns.'"

When he was just three, his mother's diary contains this entry:—

"Mr. Swan at dinner. Smout recited the first four lines of 'On Linden' in great style, waving his hand and making a splendid bow at the end. This is Cummie's teaching." And no doubt the trick of gesture, partly inherited from his father, which accompanied his conversation through life, received some of its emphasis from his nurse.

The diary just quoted records somewhat irregularly the development of the boy's powers and tastes and the working of his mind in childhood, but the nature and interest of the entries are fairly represented by the following extracts:—

"*26th July, 1853.*— Smout's favourite occupation is making a church; he makes a pulpit with a chair and a stool; reads sitting, and then stands up and sings by turns.

"*1st October, 1853.*— He is a great chatterbox, and speaks very distinctly; he knows many stories out of the Bible, and about half of the letters of the alphabet, but he is not so fond of hymns as he used to be.

"*6th November, 1853.*— I read the story of Samson once or twice out of the Bible to Smout, and was much surprised by his repeating it almost word for word.

"*8th December, 1854.*— Lou said, 'You can never be good unless you pray.' When asked how he knew, he said with great emphasis, 'Because I 've tried it.'

"*22nd December, 1854.*— Lou prays every night of

his own accord that God would bless 'the poor soldiers that are fighting at Sebastopol.'

"*25th December, 1854.*— Smout gets a sword for his Christmas present. When his father was disparaging it, he said, 'I can tell you, papa, it's a silver sword and a gold sheath, and the boy's very well off and quite contented.'

"*9th January, 1855.*— When made to wear a shawl above his sword, he was in distress for fear it would not look like a soldier, and then said, 'Do you think it will look like a night-march, mama?'

"*6th February, 1855.*— Lou dreamed that he heard 'the noise of pens writing.'

"*17th February, 1855, Sunday.*— When I asked Lou what he had been doing, he said, 'I've been playing all day,' and then when I looked at him, he added, 'at least, I've been making myself cheerful.'

"*18th April, 1856.*— Smout can't understand the days getting longer, and says he 'would rather go to bed at the seven o'clock that used to be.'

"*17th July, 1856.*— I heard to-day that what had made Smout so ill on the 5th was that he and Billy had been eating buttercups, which are poisonous; both were ill, so we may be thankful that they were not worse. Billy confessed, and Smout acknowledged whenever he was asked." (Mrs. Stevenson, however, omits the true explanation — that the boys were shipwrecked sailors, and could get no other food to support life.)

It was in the end of 1856 that Louis was for the first time experiencing "the toils and vigils and distresses" of composition. His uncle, David Stevenson, offered to his children and nephews a prize for the best history of Moses. Louis was allowed to try for it by dictating his version to his mother, and to this he devoted five successive Sunday evenings. A Bible picture-book was given to him as an extra prize, and, adds his mother, "from that time forward it was the desire of his heart to be an author."

For this he had already a qualification, which children either seldom possess, or of which at any rate they but seldom remember the possession. In a late reminiscence[1] he greatly applauds his nurse's ear and speaks of her reading to him "the works of others as a poet would scarce dare to read his own; gloating on the rhythm, dwelling with delight on the assonances and alliterations." So he tells us of the delight he already took in words for their own sake, and of the thrill which the mere sound of "Jehovah Tsidkenu" produced in him without reference to any possible meaning. To the same source I must refer for his account of the imagery called up in his mind from local surroundings by the metrical version of the Twenty-third Psalm; the "pastures green" being stubble-fields by the Water of Leith, and "death's dark vale" a certain archway in the Warriston Cemetery.

But in these suburbs only a part of his childhood was spent. Of other and happier playing-places he has left two records; the one a brief reference, with which the first description of his Edinburgh life, already quoted, terminates; the other, much more detailed, was written probably about 1872, and was manifestly the quarry from which was drawn most of the material for "The Manse" in *Memories and Portraits*.

[1] "Rosa quo Locorum," *Juvenilia*, pp. 303, 308.

46

From these two essays it may be seen that Stevenson, alike at two-and-twenty and at five-and-thirty, remembered his childhood as it is given to few grown men and women to remember, and both papers contain the raw material or perhaps rather the prose version of many passages in the *Child's Garden of Verses.*

"One consequence of my ill-health was my frequent residence at Colinton Manse. Out of my reminiscences of life in that dear place, all the morbid and painful elements have disappeared. I remember no more nights of storm; no more terror or sickness. Beyond a thunder-storm when I was frightened, after a half make-believe fashion, and huddled with my cousins underneath the dining-room table; and a great flood of the river, to see which my father carried me wrapped in a blanket through the rain; I can recall nothing but sunshiny weather. That was my golden age: *et ego in Arcadia vixi.* There is something so fresh and wholesome about all that went on at Colinton, compared with what I recollect of the town, that I can hardly, even in my own mind, knit the two chains of reminiscences together; they look like stories of two different people, ages apart in time and quite dissimilar in character." [1]

In the "Reminiscences of Colinton Manse," [2] "I take pleasure," he says, "in writing down these recollections, not because I fear to forget them, but because I wish to renew and to taste more fully the satisfaction that they have afforded me already.

"The Water of Leith, after passing under Colinton

[1] Dated Swanston, Sunday, 18th May, 1873.

[2] Unpublished MS., written probably about 1872-73.

Bridge, makes a curve, following the line of the high, steep, wooded bank on the convex, but on the concave enclosing a round flat promontory, which was once, I suppose, a marsh, and then a riverside meadow. . . . Immediately after crossing the bridge the roadway forks into two; one branch whereof tends upward to the entrance of the churchyard; while the other, green with grass, slopes downward, between two blank walls and past the cottage of the snuff-mill, to the gate of the manse.

"There were two ways of entering the manse garden: one the two-winged gate that admitted the old phaeton, and the other a door for pedestrians on the side next the kirk. . . . On the left hand were the stable, coach-house, and washing-houses, clustered round a small paven court. For the interior of these buildings, as abutting on the place of sepulture, I had always considerable terror; but the court has one pleasant memento of its own. When the grass was cut and stacked against the wall in the small paven court at the back of the house, do you not remember, my friends, making round holes in the cool, green herb and calling ourselves birds? It did not take a great height, in those days, to lift our feet off the ground; so when we shut our eyes, we were free to imagine ourselves in the fork of an elm bough, or half-way down a cliff among a colony of gulls and gannets. . . .

"Once past the stable you were now fairly within the garden. On summer afternoons the sloping lawn was literally *steeped* in sunshine; and all the day long, from the impending wood, there came the sweetest and fullest chorus of merles and thrushes and all manner of

48

birds, that it ever was my lot to hear. The lawn was
just the centre of all this — a perfect goblet for sunshine,
and the Dionysius' ear for a whole forest of bird-songs.
This lawn was a favourite playground; a lilac that hung
its scented blossom out of the glossy semicirque of lau-
rels was identified by my playmates and myself as that
tree whose very shadow was death. In the great laurel at the corner I have often lain *perdu*, with a toy-gun
in my hand, waiting for a herd of antelopes to defile
past me down the carriage drive, and waiting (need I
add ?) in vain.[1] Down at the corner of the lawn next
the snuff-mill wall there was a practicable passage
through the evergreens and a door in the wall, which
let you out on a small patch of sand, left in the corner
by the river. Just across, the woods rose like a wall
into the sky; and their lowest branches trailed in the
black waters. Naturally, it was very sunless. . . .
There was nothing around and above you but the
shadowy foliage of trees. It seemed a marvel how they
clung to the steep slope on the other side; and, indeed,
they were forced to grow far apart, and showed the
ground between them hid by an undergrowth of but-
ter-bur, hemlock, and nettle. . . . I wish I could give
you an idea of this place, of the gloom, of the black
slow water, of the strange wet smell, of the draggled

[1] Another version runs: "Once as I lay, playing hunter, hid in a
thick laurel, and with a toy-gun upon my arm, I worked myself so
hotly into the spirit of my play, that I think I can still see the herd of
antelope come sweeping down the lawn and round the deodar; it was
almost a vision."

In 1857, at Bridge of Allan, he was one day asked, "What are you
doing ?" "Ah 'm just hunting blaauwboks!"

vegetation on the far side whither the current took everything, and of the incomparably fine, rich yellow sand, without a grit in the whole of it, and moving below your feet with scarcely more resistance than a liquid. . . . I remember climbing down one day to a place where we discovered an island of this treacherous material. O the great discovery! On we leapt in a moment; but on feeling the wet, sluicy island flatten out into a level with the river, and the brown water gathering about our feet, we were off it again as quickly. It was a 'quicksand,' we said; and thenceforward the island was held in much the same regard as the lilac-tree on the lawn.

"The wall of the church faces to the manse, but the churchyard is on a level with the top of the wall, that is to say, some eight or ten feet above the garden, and the tombstones are visible from the enclosure of the manse. The church, with its campanile, was near the edge, so that on Sundays we could see the cluster of people about the door. Under the retaining wall was a somewhat dark pathway, extending from the stable to the far end of the garden, and called 'The Witches' Walk,' from a game we used to play in it. At the stable end it took its rise under a yew, which is one of the glories of the village. Under the circuit of its wide, black branches, it was always dark and cool, and there was a green scurf over all the trunk among which glistened the round bright drops of resin. . . . This was a sufficiently gloomy commencement for the Witches' Walk; but its chief horror was the retaining wall of the kirkyard itself, about which we were always hovering at even with the strange attraction of fear. This it was that supplied

our Arcady with its gods; and in place of classic forms
and the split hooves of satyrs, we were full of homely
Scottish superstitions of grues and ghosts and goblins.
. . . Often after nightfall have I looked long and eagerly from the manse windows to see the 'spunkies'
playing among the graves, and have been much chagrined at my failure ; and this very name of spunkie
recalls to me the most important of our discoveries in
the supernatural walk.   Henrietta, Willie,[1] and I, just
about dusk, discovered a burning eye looking out from
a hole in the retaining wall, in the corner where it joins
the back of the stable.   In hushed tones we debated
the question; whether it was some bird of ill omen
roosting in the cranny of the wall, or whether the hole
pierced right through into a grave, and it was some
dead man who was sitting up in his coffin and watching us with that strange fixed eye.   If you remember
the level of the churchyard, you will see that this explanation suited pretty well; so we drew a wheelbar-
row into the corner; one after another got up and looked
in; and when the last was satisfied, we turned round,
took to our heels, and never stopped till we were in
the shelter of the house.   We ourselves, in our after-
discussions, thought it might have been the bird, though
we preferred the more tremendous explanation.   But
for my own part, I simply believe that we saw nothing
at all.   The fact is, we would have given anything to
have seen a ghost, or to persuade ourselves that we
had seen a ghost. . . . I remember going down into
the cellars of our own house in town, in company with

[1] Cf. *A Child's Garden of Verses*, Envoy I.   His two favourite
cousins, the children of his mother's sister, Mrs. Ramsay Traquair.

another, . . . and persuading myself that I saw a face looking at me from round a corner; and I may even confess, since the laws against sorcery have been for some time in abeyance, that I essayed at divers times to bring up the Devil, founding my incantations on no more abstruse a guide than Skelt's *Juvenile Drama of Der Freischütz*. I am about at the end of horrors now; even out of the Witches' Walk, you saw the manse facing towards you, with its back to the river and the wooded bank, and the bright flower-plots and stretches of comfortable vegetables in front and on each side of it; flower-plots and vegetable borders, by the way, on which it was almost death to set foot, and about which we held a curious belief — namely, that my grandfather went round and measured any footprints that he saw to compare the measurement at night with the boots put out for brushing; to avoid which we were accustomed, by a strategic movement of the foot, to make the mark longer. . . .

"So much for the garden; now follow me into the house. On entering by the front door you had before you a stone-paved lobby, with doors on either hand, that extended the whole length of the house. There stood a case of foreign birds, two or three marble deities from India, and a lily of the Nile in a pot; and at the far end the stairs shut in the view. . . . With how many games of 'tig' or brick-building in the forenoon is the long low dining-room connected in my mind!

. . . "But that room is principally dear to me from memories of the time when I, a sickly child, stayed there alone. First, in the forenoon about eleven, how my aunt ˙ used to open the storeroom at the one end and give me out three Albert biscuits and some calf-foot jelly in a black pot with a sort of raised white pattern over it. That storeroom was a most voluptuous place with its piles of biscuit boxes and spice tins, the rack for buttered eggs, the little window that let in sunshine and the flickering shadow of leaves, and the strong sweet odour of everything that pleaseth the taste of man. . . . But after my biscuits were eaten and my pot emptied (I am supposing one of those many days when I was not allowed to cross the threshold), what did there remain to do? . . . I would often get some one for amanuensis, and write pleasant narratives, which have fallen some degree into unjust oblivion. One, I remember, had for scene the Witches' Walk, and for heroine a kitten. It was intended to be something very thrilling and spectral; but I can now only recall the intense satisfaction (I illustrated these works my-self) with which I contemplated three coats of gamboge upon the cat's supper of pease-brose. Another story was entitled *The Adventures of Basil*, and consisted mainly of bungling adaptations from Mayne Reid, to whom I was indebted even for my hero's name; but I

1 " I have mentioned my aunt. In her youth she was a wit and a beauty, very imperious, managing, and self-sufficient. But as she grew up, she began to suffice for all the family as well. An accident on horseback made her nearly deaf and blind, and suddenly trans-formed this wilful empress into the most serviceable and amiable of women. There were thirteen of the Balfours as (oddly enough) there were of the Stevensons also, and the children of the family came home to her to be nursed, to be educated, to be mothered, from the infanti-cidal climate of India. There must sometimes have been half a score of us children about the manse; and all were born a second time from

53

introduced the further attraction of a storm at sea, where the captain cried out, 'All hands to the pumps.' . . .

"Another time my aunt had brought me a large box of tin soldiers from town. I had only to drop the smallest hint of what I wanted and I had it the next time the phaeton went in. . . . So after dinner on the first day of my new acquisition, I was told to exhibit my soldiers to grandpapa. The idea of this great and alarming dignitary stooping to examine my toys was a new one; and I ranged my wooden militia with excessive care upon the broad mahogany, while my grandfather took his usual nuts and port wine. Not only was he pleased to approve of the way in which I had 'marshalled my array'; but he also gave a new light to me on the subject of playing with soldiers — a technical term, you observe. He told me to make the battle of Coburg. Now Waterloo I knew; and Crimean battlefields I knew (for they were within my own memory); but this Coburg was a new and grand idea, a novel vista of entertainment, an addition to my vocabulary of warlike sports; and so I have never forgotten it.

Aunt Jane's tenderness. It was strange when a new party of these sallow young folk came home, perhaps with an Indian ayah. This little country manse was the centre of the world; and Aunt Jane represented Charity. The text, my mother says, must have been written for her and Aunt Jane: 'More are the children of the barren than the children of the married wife.'"— From an autobiographical fragment, written in San Francisco early in 1880. (For other portions *vide* pages 99, 102. For the use of this I am indebted to Mrs. Strong, to whom the early part of this manuscript was presented at Vailima by her stepfather.) Cf. *Child's Garden*, Envoy III.

" But now I come to the crown of my dining-room reminiscences, for after dinner, when the lamp was brought in and shaded, and my aunt sat down to read in the rocking-chair, there was a great open space behind the sofa left entirely in the shadow. This was my especial domain: once round the corner of the sofa, I had left the lightsome, merry indoors, and was out in the cool, dark night. I could almost see the stars. I looked out of the back window at the bushes outside. I lay in the darkest corners, rifle in hand, like a hunter in a lonely bivouac. I crawled about stealthily, watching the people in the circle of lamplight, with some vague remembrance of a novel that my aunt had read to me, where some fellow went out from ' the heated ballroom ' and moralised in the ' Park.' [1] Down in the corner beside the bricks, whether on the floor or on a book-shelf I do not remember, were four volumes of Joanna Baillie's plays. Now as Cummie always expatiated on the wickedness of anything theatrical, I supposed these books to be forbidden, and took every sly opportunity of reading them. But I don't think I ever read one through: my chief satisfaction was puzzling out, in the obscurity, the scenes—' a convent in a forest: the chapel lit: organ playing a solemn chant '—' a passage in a Saxon castle ' — and the like; and then transforming my dark place behind the sofa into one and all of these. . . .

" Opposite the study was the parlour, a small room crammed full of furniture and covered with portraits, with a cabinet at the one side full of foreign curiosities, and a sort of anatomical trophy on the top. During a

[1] Cf. " A Gossip on Romance," *Memories and Portraits*, p. 249.

grand cleaning of this apartment I remember all the furniture was ranged on the circular grass-plot between the churchyard and the house. It was a lovely still summer evening, and I stayed out, climbing among the chairs and sofas. Falling on a large bone or skull, I asked what it was. Part of an albatross, auntie told me. 'What is an albatross?' I asked. And then she described to me this great bird nearly as big as a house, that you saw out miles away from any land, sleeping above the waste and desolate ocean. She told me that the *Ancient Mariner* was all about one; and quoted with great *verve* (she had a duster in her hand, I recollect) —

> ' With my crossbow
> I shot the albatross.'

"Wonderful visions did all this raise in my imagination, so wonderful, that when, many years later, I came to read the poem, my only feeling was one of utter disappointment. Willie had a crossbow; but up till this date, I had never envied him its possession. After this, however, it became one of the objects of my life."

His mother and his nurse read to him, as we have seen, indefatigably, and so it was not until he was eight years old that he took any pleasure in reading to himself. The consciousness of this delight came upon him suddenly; its coming was connected in his memory with a book called *Paul Blake*, "a visit to the country, and an experience unforgettable. The day had been warm; Henrietta and I had played together charmingly all day in a sandy wilderness across the road; then came the evening with a great flash of colour and a heavenly sweetness in the air. Somehow my playmate had vanished, or is out of the story, as the sagas say, but I was sent into the village on an errand; and taking a book of fairy-tales, went down alone through a fir-wood, reading as I walked. How often since then has it befallen me to be happy even so; but that was the first time: the shock of that pleasure I have never since forgot, and if my mind serves me to the last, I never shall; for it was then that I knew that I loved reading."[1]

This day must have been followed closely by the evening recorded in another essay.[2] "Out of all the years of my life I can recall but one home-coming to compare with these (when he returned with some new play for his toy-theatre), and that was on the night when I brought back with me the *Arabian Entertainments* in the fat, old, double-columned volume with the prints. I was just well into the story of the Hunch-back, I remember, when my clergyman grandfather (a man we counted pretty stiff) came in behind me. I grew blind with terror. But instead of ordering the book away, he said he envied me. Ah, well he might."

Although an only child and rendered more solitary by illness, Louis was not without companions, drawn (as often happens in early years) chiefly from the crowded ranks of his cousins, of whom he was nearly sure to find some at Colinton.[3] By them he seems to have been treated, as Mr. Colvin so happily says, "as

---

[1] "Rosa quo Locorum," *Juvenilia*, p. 307.

[2] "A Penny Plain and Twopence Coloured," *Memories and Portraits*, p. 288.

[3] He had more than fifty first cousins in all, forty being on his mother's side. Many of them were much younger than himself, but nearly all were born or bred in the neighbourhood of Edinburgh.

something of a small sickly prince"; over them he cast
the spell of his imagination in devising games, and they
submitted to the force of his character in accepting the
rôles which he saw fit to allot. "We children had
naturally many plays together," he says of Colinton;
"I usually insisted on the lead, and was invariably exhausted to death by the evening. I can still remember
what a fury of play would descend upon me." Whether
solitary or in company, he could never be still, but always must follow out his fancies in action. Were a
horse to be mounted, a ship to be handled, a dragon to
be slain, each and all of these operations must be con-
ducted with all the fire and fury which the very idea
aroused in his imagination.[1]

The country and the summer months gave him more
companions, but the whole winter of 1856–57 was
spent in Heriot Row by the most brilliant of them all,
the one who had most in common with Louis, and
of all his kin was his closest friend in after-life, Robert
Alan Mowbray Stevenson, the only son of his uncle
Alan. He was the cousin of "Child's Play,"[2] who ate
his porridge "with sugar, and explained it to be a country continually buried under snow," while Louis took
his "with milk, and explained it to be a country suffering gradual inundation."

"We lived together in a purely visionary state," wrote
Louis, "and were never tired of dressing up." One of
their chief delights was in the rival kingdoms of their
own invention — Nosingtonia and Encyclopædia, of
which they were perpetually drawing maps. Nosing-

[1] " Child's Play," *Virginibus Puerisque*, p. 162.
[2] P. 167. See this volume, p. 104 n.

tonia was "shaped a little like Ireland"; Encyclopædia, Louis' island, "lay diagonally across the paper like a large tip-cat." I have before me a state-paper of the period; the Latin must be the elder boy's, as Louis had not yet been to school: "Received by me from Rex Encyclopædiæ: patent thickness 1 Air Gun of Grundrungia cloth and 1000 yards therefore in exchange for the Pine Islands.—R. Stevenson, Rex Nozzinton."

It was during this winter and in this company that Louis, at the age of six, first entered the realms of gold described in "A Penny Plain and Twopence Coloured" (*Memories and Portraits*), the region of the toy-theatre and the "scenery of Skeltdom." The romance of purchasing the plays for himself came a little later, for during these months he could hardly leave the house; but now began the delight in the book and the *dramatis personæ*. Years afterwards he described himself as "no melodramatist, but a Skelt-drunken boy; the man who went out to find the Eldorado of romantic comedy." Now also began the joys of illumination. Now he painted the characters "with crimson-lake (hark to the sound of it — crimson-lake! — the horns of elf-land are not richer on the ear)—with crimson-lake and Prussian blue a certain purple is to be compounded, which, for cloaks especially, Titian could not equal."

The last of his reminiscences of childish days that I have to give was written in Samoa, and describes with all the resources of his perfected art a state of mind more subtle and tragic than any that we are accustomed to associate with the confines of infancy. From any one who less accurately remembered the sensations of his earliest years, it might seem fanciful and unreal; to those who know the truthfulness with which its author has depicted the successive stages through which he passed, it will be as convincing as it is delightful.   On this page also we first meet his sentiment for the venerable city which to the end he thought of as his home.

"I was born within the walls of that dear city of Zeus,[1] of which the lightest and (when he chooses) the tenderest singer of my generation sings so well. I was born likewise within the bounds of an earthly city, illustrious for her beauty, her tragic and picturesque associations, and for the credit of some of her brave sons. Writing as I do in a strange quarter of the world, and a late day of my age, I can still behold the profile of her towers and chimneys, and the long trail of her smoke against the sunset; I can still hear those strains of martial music that she goes to bed with, ending each day, like an act of an opera, to the notes of bugles; still recall, with a grateful effort of memory, any one of a thousand beautiful and specious circumstances that pleased me, and that must have pleased any one, in my half-remembered past. It is the beautiful that I thus actively recall: the august airs of the castle on its rock, nocturnal passages of lights and trees, the sudden song of the blackbird in a suburban lane, rosy and dusky winter sunsets, the uninhabited splendours of the early

[1] The reference is to "Seekers for a City" in the volume of poems by Mr. Andrew Lang, entitled *Grass of Parnassus* (London : Longmans & Co., 1888).   The quotation prefixed to the poem is from the *Meditations of Marcus Aurelius*, iv. 19.   "The poet says, *dear city of Cecrops*, and wilt not thou say, *dear city of Zeus?*"

dawn, the building up of the city on a misty day, house above house, spire above spire, until it was received into a sky of softly glowing clouds, and seemed to pass on and upwards, by fresh grades and rises, city beyond city, a New Jerusalem, bodily scaling heaven. . . .

"Memory supplies me, unsolicited, with a mass of other material, where there is nothing to call beauty, nothing to attract — often a great deal to disgust. There are trite street corners, commonplace, well-to-do houses, shabby suburban tan-fields, rainy beggarly slums, taken in at a gulp nigh forty years ago, and surviving to-day, complete sensations, concrete, poignant and essential to the genius of the place. From the melancholy of these remembrances I might suppose them to belong to the wild and bitterly unhappy days of my youth. But it is not so; they date, most of them, from early childhood; they were observed as I walked with my nurse, gaping on the universe, and striving vainly to piece together in words my inarticulate but profound impressions. I seem to have been born with a sentiment of something moving in things of an infinite attraction and horror coupled."

CHAPTER IV

BOYHOOD — 1859–67

" Not all roads lead to Rome — only that you have begun to travel."
—R. L. S.

IT was not till 1859 that the boy's continuous school-
ing began, but to his formal education little or no importance attaches. The changes of his teachers were
frequent, his absences from school innumerable, but
both were due almost entirely to his health, and especially his susceptibility to colds. In the autumn of
1857 he had gone to Mr. Henderson's preparatory
school in India Street, in the near neighbourhood of his
home, as all his day-schools were. After a few weeks
he had to give it up, and did not return there till October, 1859. In 1861 he was transferred to the Edinburgh
Academy, then, as now, the leading school of Edinburgh;
there he spent a year and a half under Mr. D'Arcy Went-
worth Thompson, author of *Day-Dreams of a School-
master* and other works, a teacher with views far in
advance of his day, and now for many years Professor
of Greek in the Queen's College, Galway. Then for
one term, his mother being abroad, he was sent to an
English boarding-school at Spring Grove, Isleworth, in
Middlesex. Finally, in 1864, he was again shifted —
to a day-school kept by Mr. Thomson in Frederick
Street, Edinburgh, which he attended with more or less
regularity until he went to the University in 1867.

Besides his ordinary classes he had many tutors for

longer or shorter periods, in Edinburgh and elsewhere, both when he was unable to leave the house, and also in order to supplement and help his school-work, a custom prevalent in Scotland.

It is only of his experiences at his last two schools that anything definite seems to be remembered. The Spring Grove establishment has little interest for us beyond having been his only boarding-school and the source of his remarks on English schoolboys in "The Foreigner at Home."[1] He left home for Isleworth with mixed feelings, and of his breakdown before he went, and of "the benevolent cat" that "cumbered him with consolations" on a doorstep, he has told us in "Random Memories."[2] His misgivings were on the whole justified by the event, for the school seems to have been rather a nondescript place. A list given in one of his letters includes two parlour-boarders, three big boys, six of "midling size," of whom "Stevenson" was one, and the enumeration ends with "small-fry lots." For the only time in his life he joined in games, he collected coins, and he wrote letters to his parents full of drawings, eked out with fragments of Latin exercises and attempts at French. His aunt had left Colinton, and was now living at Spring Grove, in charge of other nephews who attended the same school, and to her house he was often allowed to go. But he had been told to let his father know if he were not happy, and although he stayed to the end of the quarter, he then secured a promise that he should not again be sent from home.

Of Mr. Thomson's school we have an account from

[1] The first paper in *Memories and Portraits*.   [2] *Ibid.*, p. 289.

Mr. H. Bellyse Baildon,[1] who was a pupil there during the same years.[2]

"I do not think there were at this little seminary more than a dozen boys, ranging in ages from nine or ten to fourteen or fifteen, and our intellectual calibre varied fully as much as our years. For some of us were sent there for reasons of health, and others because they had not made that progress with their studies which their fond parents had hoped. Others were there, I fancy, because the scheme of education upon which the proprietor, Mr. Robert Thomson, proceeded fell in with the views of our parents. The main feature of this system was, so far as I can recollect, that we had no home lessons, but learned, in the two or three hours of afternoon school, what we were expected to remember next day.

"Our freedom from home tasks gave us leisure for literary activities which would otherwise have been tabooed as waste of time. Perhaps with some of us they were, but not with Stevenson. For even then he had a fixed idea that literature was his calling, and a marvellously mature conception of the course of self-education through which he required to put himself in order to succeed. Among other things we were encouraged to make verse translations, and for some reason or other, I specially well remember a passage of Ovid, which he rendered in Scott-like octosyllabics, and I in heroic couplets, which I probably thought com-

[1] Sometime Lecturer on the English Language and Literature in the University of Vienna.

[2] *Temple Bar*, March, 1895 ; also *Robert Louis Stevenson : a Life Study in Criticism*, by H. Bellyse Baildon (Chatto and Windus, 1901).

mendably like those of Mr. Pope. But, even then, Stevenson showed impatience of the trammels of verse, and longed for the compass and ductility of prose."

The teachers who gave him private lessons spoke of his intelligence in high terms, but in large classes he evaded the eye of the master and drew on himself as little notice as possible. The Reverend Peter Rutherford, who taught him when he was at Mr. Henderson's, says: "He was without exception the most delightful boy I ever knew; full of fun, full of tender feeling; ready for his lessons, ready for a story, ready for fun"; and the master of the Burgh School at Peebles, who gave him lessons in 1864, found him the most intelligent and best-informed boy in all his experience. A glowing interest in any subject that took his fancy marked his earliest boyhood no less than his later years. But if he was bright and ready when he was interested, his attention was often short-lived, and to many of the subjects in his curriculum it never was given at all. In every language that he ever learned, the rules of its grammar remained unknown to him, however correctly he might use its idioms, and the spelling of his own tongue was dark to nim to the very last. Latin, French, and mathematics seem to have been everywhere the staple of his education. German he began with a private tutor in 1865 at Torquay, where he also received his only lessons in ordinary drawing. The only prize that ever fell to him was at Mr. Henderson's school for his reading, which was commended, as he tells us, with the criticism: "Robert's voice, though not strong, is impressive." [1]

[1] *Juvenilia*, p. 308.

On the physical side of his education, dancing, despite the Covenanters, was persistently taught him with but scanty success: riding he learned chiefly in the summers of 1865 and 1866, though he first had a pony in 1856. In 1860 and 1864 he was bathing with great enjoyment, and in the latter year he was also rowing on the Tweed. But of games proper there is little mention. From Spring Grove he wrote: "Yesterday I was playing at football. I have never played at cricket, so papa may comfort himself with that. I like football very much." Against this we have to set his confession that even at football "I knew at least one little boy who was mightily exercised about the presence of the ball, and had to spirit himself up, whenever he came to play, with an elaborate story of enchantment, and take the missile as a sort of talisman bandied about in conflict between two Arabian nations."[1] And at North Berwick he says: "You might golf if you wanted, but I seem to have been better employed."[2]

But if his health were unequal to constant schoolwork or severe exercise, it greatly improved after 1863, and did not disable him from other boyish pursuits. Already, in 1857, his mother had written: "Louis is getting very wild and like a boy." In 1864 she records that "Whatever there was in him of 'Puck'[3] came very much to the front this summer. He was the leader of a number of boys who went about playing tricks on all the neighbours on Springhill, tapping on their windows after nightfall," and all manner of wild freaks.

[1] "Child's Play," p. 168.
[2] *Additional Memories and Portraits*, p. 349.　　　[3] See p. 376.

The following year at Peebles he became a reckless rider. A girl companion of those days recollects the time "when my brother Bob, Louis, and I used to ride together. Bob had a black pony, and Louis called it 'Hell'; his own was brown, and was called 'Purgatory'; while mine was named 'Heaven.' Once the two boys galloped right through the Tweed on the way to Innerleithen, and I had to follow in fear of my life — poor 'Heaven' had the worst of it on that occasion."

"In this year, too," says Louis himself, "at the ripe age of fourteen years, I bought a certain cudgel, got a friend to load it, and thenceforward walked the tame ways of the earth my own ideal, radiating pure romance — still but a puppet in the hand of Skelt." [1]

Nor was another element wanting. He speaks of Neidpath Castle in the close vicinity of Peebles, "bosomed in hills on a green promontory: Tweed at its base running through the gamut of a busy river, from the pouring shallow to the brown pool. In the days when I was thereabouts, that part of the earth was made a heaven to me by many things now lost, by boats and bathing, and the fascination of streams, and the delights of comradeship and those (surely the prettiest and simplest) of a boy and girl romance." [2]

Earlier experiences belonging to North Berwick and the autumn of 1862 are described in *Memories and Portraits;* [3] these included fishing, bathing, wading, and "crusoeing" — "a word that covers all extempore eating in the open air: digging, perhaps, a house under

---

[1] "A Penny Plain and Twopence Coloured," p. 232.
[2] *Scribner's Magazine*, July, 1888, p. 125.   [3] Pp. 349, 353.

the margin of the links, kindling a fire of the sea-ware and cooking apples there." But the crown of all was the business of the lantern-bearers, a sport which was afterwards to Stevenson the type of all that was anti-realist and romantic.

"Toward the end of September, when school-time was drawing near and the nights were already black, we would begin to sally from our respective villas, each equipped with a tin bull's-eye lantern. The thing was so well known that it had worn a rut in the commerce of Great Britain; and the grocers, about the due time, began to garnish their windows with our particular brand of luminary. We wore them buckled to the waist upon a cricket belt, and over them, such was the rigour of the game, a buttoned top-coat. They smelled noisomely of blistered tin; they never burned aright, though they would always burn our fingers; their use was naught; the pleasure of them merely fanciful; and yet a boy with a bull's-eye under his top-coat asked for nothing more. The fishermen used lanterns about their boats, and it was from them, I suppose, that we had got the hint; but theirs were not bull's-eyes, nor did we ever play at being fishermen. The police carried them at their belts, and we had plainly copied them in that; yet we did not pretend to be policemen. Burglars, indeed, we may have had some haunting thoughts of; and we certainly had an eye to past ages when lanterns were more common, to certain story-books in which we had found them to figure very largely. But take it for all in all, the pleasure of the thing was substantive; and to be a boy with a bull's-eye under his top-coat was good enough for us.

"When two of these asses met, there would be an anxious 'Have you got your lantern?' and a gratified 'Yes.' That was the shibboleth, and very needful, too; for, as it was the rule to keep our glory contained, none could recognise a lantern-bearer, unless (like a polecat) by the smell. Four or five would sometimes climb into the belly of a ten-man lugger, with nothing but the thwarts above them—for the cabin was usually locked — or choose out some hollow of the links where the wind might whistle overhead. There the coats would be unbuttoned and the bull's-eyes discovered; and in the chequering glimmer, under the huge windy hall of the night, and cheered by a rich steam of toasting tinware, these fortunate young gentlemen would crouch together in the cold sand of the links or on the scaly bilges of the fishing-boat, and delight themselves with inappropriate talk.

"Woe is me that I may not give some specimens — some of their foresights of life, or deep inquiries into the rudiments of man and nature — these were so fiery and so innocent, they were so richly silly, so romantically young. But the talk, at any rate, was but a condiment; and these gatherings themselves only accidents in the career of the lantern-bearer. The essence of this bliss was to walk by yourself in the black night; the slide shut, the top-coat buttoned; not a ray escaping, whether to conduct your footsteps or to make your glory public: a mere pillar of darkness in the dark; and all the while, deep down in the privacy of your fool's heart, to know you had a bull's-eye at your belt, and to exult and sing over the knowledge."

Meanwhile, apart from his schools, the boy was gaining a wider knowledge of the world and having his first experiences of travel. In Scotland his long summer holidays were spent in the country much as before, until the manse at Colinton began to "shield a stranger race." Now at some time he paid a visit to one of his uncles in the parish of Stow, on which, perhaps, he afterwards drew in *Weir of Hermiston* for his knowledge of the Lammermuirs. In 1857 he had crossed the Border with his parents for the first time, and visited the English Lakes. In 1862, the year of the second International Exhibition, his father's health brought the family to London and the South of England, and Louis saw not only the sights of the capital, but also Salisbury, Stonehenge, and the Isle of Wight. In July the same cause took them all for a month to Homburg, which Louis ‧liked very well, though he wearied sorely for the company of other boys. But this was only the beginning of his wanderings: in the winter of the same year Mrs. Stevenson was ordered to Mentone, and it was decided that her husband, her son, and a niece of Mr. Stevenson should accompany her. Thither they went in January, and there they stayed two months. In March they made a tour through Genoa, Naples, Rome, Florence, Venice, and Innsbruck, returning home by the Rhine. His mother stayed behind in England, and Louis travelled from London by himself for the first time, reaching Edinburgh on the 29th of May.

In the autumn he accompanied his father on a brief tour of lighthouse inspection in Fife, and on one day they visited seventeen lights.

At Christmas, 1863, Mrs. Stevenson was again at Mentone; there Louis joined her from his boarding-school, and they remained in the Riviera till the beginning of May. The two next springs were passed by mother and son at Torquay, but after that it proved unnecessary for them to leave Scotland for any part of the winter. For the last three winters they were joined by Miss Jessie Warden, another niece of Mr. Stevenson, a clever and original girl, just grown to womanhood. In 1867, to their great grief, she died; she had filled an important part in their small circle, had been a delightful companion to Louis, and always held a bright place in his memory.

The curious point about the foreign journeys is that they seem to have had very little manifest influence upon Stevenson, and to have passed almost entirely out of his mind. A boy of twelve, even if backward in his education, is generally a good deal impressed by experiences of this nature, and remembers them more or less distinctly throughout his life.

His cousin Mrs. Napier, who was one of the party in 1863, kindly tells me that she recollects distinctly how much he developed at this period. "In some ways," she says, "he was more like a boy of sixteen. My uncle had a great belief (inherited from his father) in the educational value of travel, and to this end and for the benefit of Louis he devoted his whole energies in the five months abroad. In the hotel at Nice he began to take Louis to the smoking-room with him; there my uncle was always surrounded by a group of eager and amused listeners — English, American, and Russian — and every subject, political, artistic, and theological, was discussed and argued. Uncle Tom's genial man-

LIFE OF ROBERT LOUIS STEVENSON

ner found friends wherever he went, and the same sort of thing went on during the whole journey. Then in regard to what we saw, his keen admiration of art and architecture seemed to be shared by Louis; they would go into raptures over a cathedral, or an old archway, or a picture. I still remember Louis' eager interest in Pompeii and in the Catacombs at Rome; Venice, too, he specially enjoyed. In some of his books there are touches which his mother and I both recognised as due to places and persons seen in that long-past journey. And in the Vailima prayers I seem to hear again an old melody that I know well — the echo of his father's words and daily devotions."

Yet nowhere, so far as I know, did Louis allude to any of the more famous towns he then visited, as if they had come within his personal ken. Mr. Horatio Brown frequently discussed Venice with him at Davos, but without even discovering that he had ever set foot in Italy. Rome meant to Stevenson in after-life a great deal: the Roman Empire was far more of a reality to him than to many better scholars and many frequenters of the city of Rome. Yet Mr. Lloyd Osbourne tells me that the only reference he ever heard his step-father make to this time was on one occasion when he recalled with delight the picturesque appearance of their military escort in horsemen's cloaks riding through the Papal States. Five years later his correspondence proves him already a keen observer, and yet half an hour with a guide-book would have furnished him with all the knowledge of Italian cities that he ever displayed.

With the country it was otherwise. "The Rhone

72

is the River of Angels," he wrote to Mr. Low; "I have adored it since I was twelve and first saw it from the train." And the scenery of *Will o' the Mill* was taken in part from the Brenner Pass, which he never saw again after 1863.

But if his stores of experience were but little increased by these changes of scene, at least the boy was learning to exercise the *savoir-faire* which came very naturally to his disposition. At hotels he used to go to the table d'hôte alone, if necessary, and made friends freely with strangers. On his return from Homburg, he made great friends on the steamer with a Dutchman, who kept saying over to himself, "I loike this booy." His French master at Mentone, on his second visit, gave him no regular lessons, but merely talked to him in French, teaching him piquet and card tricks, introducing him to various French people, and taking him to convents and other places. So his mother remarks of his other masters at home, "I think they found it pleasanter to talk to him than to teach him."

Of the other side of his character, of the solitary, dreamy, rather unhappy child, but little record survives, or little evidence which can be assigned with certainty to these years. He speaks in his essay on Pepys of the egotism of children and their delight in the anticipations of memory, as an experience of his own. "I can remember to have written in the flyleaf of more than one book the date and the place where I then was—if, for instance, I was ill in bed or sitting in a certain garden: these were jottings for my future self; if I should chance on such a note in after-years, I thought it would cause me a particular thrill to recognise myself across the intervening distance."[1]

In one of his books he touches a chord which thrills with a personal emotion as he describes "a malady most incident to only sons." "He flew his private signal and none heeded it; it seemed he was abroad in a world from which the very hope of intimacy was banished."[2] It was a slightly older lad of whom he was thinking at the moment, but the malady begins at an early age, and tends unfortunately to be chronic.

Of his appearance at this time Mr. Baildon says: "Stevenson calls himself 'ugly' in his student days, but I think this is a term that never at any time fitted him. Certainly to him as a boy of about fourteen (with the creed which he propounded to me that at sixteen one was a man) it would not apply. In body he was assuredly badly set up. His limbs were long, lean, and spidery, and his chest flat, so as almost to suggest some malnutrition, such sharp corners did his joints make under his clothes. But in his face this was belied. His brow was oval and full, over soft brown eyes that seemed already to have drunk the sunlight under Southern vines. The whole face had a tendency to an oval Madonna-like type. But about the mouth and in the mirthful mocking light of the eyes there lingered ever a ready Autolycus roguery that rather suggested sly Hermes masquerading as a mortal. The eyes were always genial, however gaily the lights danced in them, but about the mouth there was something a little tricksy and mocking, as of a spirit that

---

[1] "Pepys," *Familiar Studies of Men and Books*, p. 275.
[2] *Weir of Hermiston*, p. 155.

already peeped behind the scenes of life's pageant and more than guessed its·unrealities."

His reading progressed: for the date of his first introduction to Shakespeare there seems to be no evidence, and but for the strength of its impression it may have belonged to the earlier period. "I never supposed that a book was to command me until, one disastrous day of storm, the heaven full of turbulent vapours, the street full of the squalling of the gale, the windows resounding under bucketfuls of rain, my mother read aloud to me *Macbeth*. I cannot say I thought the experience agreeable; I far preferred the ditch-water stories that a child could dip and skip and doze over, stealing at times materials for play; it was something new and shocking to be thus ravished by a giant, and I shrank under the brutal grasp. But the spot in memory is still sensitive; nor do I ever read that tragedy but I hear the gale howling up the valley of the Leith." [1]

His first acquaintance with Dumas began in 1863 with the study of certain illustrated dessert plates in a hotel at Nice:[2] his first enthusiasm for Scott's novels belongs with certainty to the time when he had begun to select his books ior himself.

"My father's library was a spot of some austerity; the proceedings of learned societies, some Latin divinity, cyclopædias, physical science, and, above all, optics, held the chief place upon the shelves, and it was only in holes and corners that anything really legible existed as by accident. The *Parent's Assistant, Rob Roy, Waverley,* and *Guy Mannering,* the *Voyages of*

[1] *Scribner's Magazine*, July, 1888, p. 125.
[2] *Memories and Portraits*, p. 236.

Captain Woodes Rogers, Fuller's and Bunyan's *Holy Wars*, *The Reflections of Robinson Crusoe*,[1] *The Female Bluebeard*, G. Sand's *Mare au Diable* (how came it in that grave assembly!), Ainsworth's *Tower of London*, and four old volumes of *Punch* — these were the chief exceptions. In these latter, which made for years the chief of my diet, I very early fell in love (almost as soon as I could spell) with the Snob Papers. I knew them almost by heart, particularly the visit to the Pontos; and I remember my surprise when I found, long afterwards, that they were famous, and signed with a famous name; to me, as I read and admired them, they were the works of Mr. Punch. Time and again I tried to read *Rob Roy*, with whom, of course, I was acquainted from the *Tales of a Grandfather;* time and again the early part with Rashleigh and (think of it!) the adorable Diana choked me off; and I shall never forget the pleasure and surprise with which, lying on the floor one summer evening, I struck of a sudden into the first scene with Andrew Fairservice. 'The worthy Dr. Lightfoot' — 'mistrysted with a bogle'—'a wheen green trash'—'Jenny, lass, I think I ha'e her'; from that day to this the phrases have been unforgotten. I read on, I need scarce say; I came to Glasgow, I bided tryst on Glasgow Bridge, I met Rob Roy and the Bailie in the Tolbooth, all with transporting pleasure; and then the clouds gathered once more about my path; and I dozed and skipped until I stumbled half asleep into the Clachan of Aberfoyle, and the voices of Iverach

---

[1] *Serious Reflections during the Life and Surprising Adventures of Robinson Crusoe*. The third part of *Robinson Crusoe*, by Defoe, containing moral reflections only.

and Galbraith recalled me to myself. With that scene and the defeat of Captain Thornton the book concluded; Helen and her sons shocked even the little schoolboy of nine or ten with their unreality; I read no more, or I did not grasp what I was reading; and years elapsed before I consciously met Diana and her father among the hills, or saw Rashleigh dying in the chair. When I think of that novel and that evening, I am impatient with all others; they seem but shadows and impostors; they cannot satisfy the appetite which this awakened." [1]

What neither instruction nor travel could do for him, was none the less coming about; the boy was educating himself; learning to write patiently, persistently, without brilliance or any apparent prospect of success. The History of Moses of 1856 had been followed the next year by a History of Joseph, after a brief interval devoted to a story "in slavish imitation of Mayne Reid." Two years later came an account (still dictated) of his travels in Perth. Before thirteen he wrote a description of the inhabitants of Peebles in the style of the *Book of Snobs*. When he was fourteen he developed a facility for extemporising doggerel rhymes, and composed the libretto of an opera called *The Baneful Potato*, of which only the names of two characters survive — "Dig-him-up-o," the gardener, and "Seek-him-out-o," the policeman, and the first line of an aria sung by the heroine, "My own dear casement window."

At his last school and in his home circle he was always starting magazines. These were all in manuscript, generally illustrated with profusion of colour,

[1] "Rosa quo Locorum," *Juvenilia*, p. 310.

and were sometimes circulated at a charge of one penny for reading. *The Schoolboys' Magazine* of 1863, of which one number survives, contained four stories, and its readers must have been hard to satisfy if they did not have their fill of horrors. In the first tale, "The Adventures of Jan van Steen," the hero is left hidden in a boiler under which a fire is lit. The second is "A Ghost Story" of robbers in a deserted castle in "one of those barren places called plains in the north of Norway." A traveller finds a man, "half killed with several wounds," hidden under the floor, who dresses up as a ghost. The third story is called, by a curious anticipation, "The Wreckers." On the shore at North Berwick "were two men. The older and stronger of the two was a tall, ill-looking man with grizzled hair and a red nose. He was dressed in a tarnished gold-laced blue coat, a red waistcoat, and leggings. The other, who might have been a fisherman except for the fact that from each of the pockets of his pea-jacket there projected a pistol. He was a more villainous-looking fellow than the other. 'Dan,' said the first, 'what is that clinging to that mast?' 'I think,' said the other, 'it is a sailor. You had better go and secure him.'" Last and not least terrible is "Creek Island, or Adventures in the South Seas." A line-of-battle ship called the *Shark* is wrecked in the Southern Ocean on its way to India, and two midshipmen fall into the hands of the Indians. "They had a council which pronounced death, but which death would we have to suffer? It was to be burned alive. . . . Next morning very early we had to get up and prepare to be burned alive. When we arrived at the place of execution, we shuddered to think of being killed so soon. But I forgot to tell you that I had made love to [*sic*] beautiful girl even in one day, and from all I knew she loved me. The next thing they did was to build round us sticks and rubbish of all kinds till we could hardly see what they were doing. At last they finished. They then set fire to it, and after it had got hold well, they began to dance, which is called a war-dance. (To be continued.)"

"*I forgot to tell you that I had made love to beautiful girl.*" "Was ever woman in this humour wooed?" At least the author remembered his own boyish taste, when heroines were excluded from *Treasure Island*. And yet this was the hand that at the last drew Barbara Grant and the two Kirstie Elliotts.

The Schoolboys' Magazine is, to say the least, lively reading; not so much may be claimed for "*The Sunbeam Magazine*, an illustrated Miscellany of Fact, Fiction, and Fun, edited by R. L. Stevenson," which expired in the middle of its third number in March, 1866. Each number contained several stories and articles, some evidently by other hands. The chief story, "The Banker's Ward, a modern tale," is clearly by the editor, but is a dreary and unpromising narrative of middle-class life.

In these days he had endless talks with Mr. Baildon, who seems to have been the first of his friends in whom he found a kindred interest in letters, and at one of these discussions he produced a drama which was apparently the earliest draft of *Deacon Brodie*. The story was familiar to him from childhood, as a cabinet made by the Deacon himself formed part of the furniture of his nursery. His deepest and most lasting interest was, however, centred in the Covenanters, of whom he had first learned from his nurse. He has told us how his attention was fixed on Hackston of Rathillet, who sat on horseback "with the cloak about his mouth," watching the assassination of Archbishop Sharp, in which he would take no part, lest it should be attributed to his private quarrel. Stevenson's first novel on the subject was attempted before he was fifteen, and "reams of paper," then and at a later date, were devoted to it in vain.[1]

A similar fate attended a novel on the Pentland Rising — an episode well known to him from his infancy, as the Covenanters had spent the night before their defeat in the village of Colinton.

This last composition, however, was not wholly without result. Though the novel was destroyed, his studies issued in a small green pamphlet, entitled *The Pentland Rising: a Page of History, 1666*, published anonymously, in 1866, by Andrew Elliot in Edinburgh.[2]

Miss Jane Balfour writes: "I was at Heriot Row in 1866 from the 29th October to 23rd November, and Louis was busily altering the *Pentland Rising* then to please his father. He had made a story of it, and by so doing had, in his father's opinion, spoiled it. It was printed not long after in a small edition, and Mr. Stevenson very soon bought all the copies in, as far as was possible."

Thus the period closes somewhat surprisingly with Stevenson's first appearance as a printed author. The

[1] *Additional Memories*, p. 297.
[2] List of Stevenson's works, Appendix F.

foundations were being well laid, but the structure raised upon them was premature. The publication was probably due to his father's approval of the subject-matter rather than to any belief in the literary ripeness of the style. At the same time, it was the best work that he had yet done, and the plentiful quotations from the pages of Wodrow and Kirkton, and of their opponent, Sir James Turner, are interesting in view of Stevenson's confession in Samoa,[1] "My style is from the Covenanting writers."

[1] *Letters*, ii. 312.

CHAPTER V

" Light foot, and tight foot,
　　And green grass spread,
　　Early in the morning,
　　　But hope is on ahead."
　　　　　　R. L. S.

THE time had come for the boy to leave school, and for his education to be shaped in some conformity with the profession supposed to lie before him.　What this would be was never for a moment in doubt.　Father and sons, the Stevensons were civil engineers, and to the grandsons naturally, in course of time, the business would be transferred.　The family capacity for the work, though undeniable, was very elusive, consisting chiefly of a sort of instinct for dealing with the forces of nature, and seldom manifested clearly till called forth in actual practice.　The latest recruit had certainly shown no conspicuous powers at any of his schools, but to such a criterion no one could have attached less value than his father.　That he did possess the family gift was proved before he left the profession; but even had he never written his paper " On a New Form of Intermittent Light," no one could reasonably have condemned on his behalf the choice of this career.

Accordingly, the next three and a half years were devoted to his preparation for this employment.　He spent the winter and sometimes the summer sessions at the University of Edinburgh working for a Science

82

degree, and saw something of the practical work of engineering during the other summer months.

For the first two years he attended the Latin class, Greek being abandoned as hopeless after the first session; to Natural Philosophy he was constant, so far as his constancy in such matters ever went; Mathematics then replaced Greek, and Civil Engineering took the room of Latin. But all this was none of his real education. Although he remembered that "the spinning of a top is a case of Kinetic Stability" (one of the few facts recorded in a still surviving notebook), and that "Emphyteusis is not a disease, nor Stillicide a crime," and would not willingly part with such scraps of science, he never "set the same store by them as by certain other odds and ends that he came by in the open street while he was playing truant." The last word recurs with every reference to his education. In fact, as far as the University was concerned, he "acted upon an extensive and highly rational system of truantry, which cost him a great deal of trouble to put in exercise"; and "no one ever played the truant with more deliberate care, and none ever had more certificates (of attendance) for less education."

Nor was the attention he bestowed on engineering any more assiduous. As for his practical instruction, he followed out his father's views on training—that it was waste of time for an engineer to attempt to be a craftsman in any one trade, but that he should become familiar in "shops" and yards with the materials used in his work, and should learn their employment in practice.

In the summer of 1868 Stevenson spent the month

of July at Anstruther, and the six weeks following at Wick: records of which he has left in various letters written to his parents at the time, and in the essay on "Random Memories" entitled "The Education of an Engineer." In the first-named place he was privileged to hear it said of him for the first time, "That 's the man that 's in charge." At Wick, besides his descent in a diving-suit (" one of the best things I got from my education as an engineer "), an accident afforded him one of those opportunities for prompt action, of which his life contained all too few. It comes as the post-script to a short business letter to his father.

"*September, 1868.*

"*P. S.*—I was forgetting my only news. A man fell off the staging this forenoon. I heard crying, and ran out to the end. By that time a rope had been low-ered and the man was holding himself up by it, and of course wearing himself out. Some were away for a boat. 'Hold on, Angus,' they cried. 'I can NOT do it,' he said, with wonderful composure. I told them to lower a plank; everybody was too busy giving ad-vice to listen to me; meantime the man was drowning. I was desperate, and could have knocked another dozen off. One fellow, Bain, a diver, listened to me. We got the plank out and a rope round it; but they would not help us to lower it down. At last we got assis-tance, and were just about to lower it down, when some one cried, 'Hold your hand, lads! Here comes the boat.' And Angus was borne safely in. But my hand shook so, that I could not draw for some time after with the excitement.—R. S."

He had some rough experience, but was apparently none the worse for it. "*Wick, September, 1868.*—I have had a long, hard day's work in cold, wind, and almost incessant rain. . . . We got a lighter and a boat, and were out till half-past seven, doing labourers' work, pulling, hauling, and tugging. It was past eight before I got dinner, as I was soaking, and bathed with mud to the ears; but, beyond being tired with the unusual exertion, I am all right now."

The following year he went with his father in the *Pharos*, the steamer of the Commissioners of Northern Lights, to Shetland, a part of the same cruise as that on which his grandfather had attended Sir Walter Scott. He treasured the memories of this time, but the record contained in his letters is somewhat disappointing. It was years afterwards that mentioning a boat-cloak, the use of which belonged chiefly to these days, he said: "The proudest moments of my life have been passed in the stern-sheets of a boat with that romantic garment about my shoulders. This, without prejudice to one glorious day when, standing upon some water-stairs at Lerwick, I signalled with a pocket-handkerchief for a boat to come ashore for me. I was then aged fifteen or sixteen [eighteen]. Conceive my glory."

In 1870, besides a week at Dunoon, to look after some work that was being done there, and one or two expeditions with the University engineering class, he spent three weeks on the little island of Earraid, off Mull, the scene of David Balfour's shipwreck, commemorated also in *Memories and Portraits*, but then in use as headquarters for the building of the deep-sea lighthouse of Dhu Heartach.

All this was the attractive part of his work. "As a way of life," he wrote, "I wish to speak with sympathy of my education as an engineer. It takes a man into the open air; it keeps him hanging about harbour-sides, which is the richest form of idling; it carries him to wild islands; it gives him a taste of the genial dangers of the sea; it supplies him with dexterities to exercise; it makes demands upon his ingenuity; it will go far to cure him of any taste (if he ever had one) for the miserable life of cities. And when it has done so, it carries him back and shuts him in an office. From the roaring skerry and the wet thwart of the tossing boat, he passes to the stool and desk; and with a memory full of ships, and seas, and perilous headlands, and the shining pharos, he must apply his long-sighted eyes[1] to the pretty niceties of drawing, or measure his inaccurate mind with several pages of consecutive figures. He is a wise youth, to be sure, who can balance one part of genuine life against two parts of drudgery between four walls, and for the sake of the one, manfully accept the other."[2]

But even the open-air life had only a very slight hold upon him, as far as it was devoted to professional work. Nothing could be more convincing than the little picture of his father and himself given in the *Family of Engineers*.[3]

"My father would pass hours on the beach, brooding over the waves, counting them, noting their least deflection, noting when they broke. On Tweedside, or by Lyne and Manor, we have spent together whole

---

[1] This also was his own experience.

[2] *Additional Memories and Portraits*, p. 313.   [3] P. 266.

afternoons; to me, at the time, extremely wearisome; to him, as I am now sorry to think, extremely mortifying. The river was to me a pretty and various spectacle; I could not see—I could not be made to see—it otherwise. To my father it was a chequer-board of lively forces, which he traced from pool to shallow with minute appreciation and enduring interest. ' That bank was being undercut,' he might say. ' Why? Suppose you were to put a groin out here, would not the *filum fluminis* be cast abruptly off across the channel? and where would it impinge upon the other shore? and what would be the result? Or suppose you were to blast that boulder, what would happen? Follow it—use the eyes that God has given you: can you not see that a great deal of land would be reclaimed upon this side? ' It was to me like school in holidays; but to him, until I had worn him out with my invincible triviality, a delight."

Meanwhile his life was surrounded by the ordinary material comforts belonging to his class, and the customary diversions of society were open to him, had he found them at all to his taste.

In Heriot Row he had now for his own use the two rooms on the top floor of his father's house which had been his nurseries. The smaller chamber, to the east, was his bedroom, while the other held his books, and was used as his study as long as he lived in Edinburgh.[1]

At the beginning of this period a change was made in the household arrangements, which was of material service both to his health and also to his subsequent

[1] The roof was raised and the front of the two rooms improved about 1873.

work. In May, 1867, his father took the lease of a house known as Swanston Cottage, lying in a nook at the foot of the Pentland Hills,[1] at a distance of some five miles from Edinburgh and two and a half from the boy's paradise of Colinton.

This was afterwards the home of the heroine of *St. Ives,* and in the *Picturesque Notes on Edinburgh* its situation and history were described.

"Upon the main slope of the Pentlands . . . a bouquet of old trees stands round a white farmhouse; and from a neighbouring dell you can see smoke rising and leaves rustling in the breeze. Straight above, the hills climb a thousand feet into the air. The neighbourhood, about the time of lambs, is clamorous with the bleating of flocks; and you will be awakened in the grey of early summer mornings by the barking of a dog, or the voice of a shepherd shouting to the echoes. This, with the hamlet lying behind unseen, is Swanston. . . . Long ago, this sheltered field was purchased by the Edinburgh magistrates for the sake of the springs that rise or gather there. After they had built their waterhouse and laid their pipes, it occurred to them that the place was suitable for junketing. . . . The dell was turned into a garden; and on the knoll that shelters it from the plain and the sea winds, they built a cottage looking to the hills. They brought crockets and gar-

---

[1] "I have been on a good many Scotch hills; but the competitors for the first prize are only four: Ben Lomond, Goatfell, Demyet, and Swanston (Caerketton), the eastmost of the Pentlands. . . . Considering the beauty of Edinburgh, and the dignity imparted to scenery by objects of importance, I am rather inclined to give the palm to that Pentland." — Lord Cockburn, *Circuit Journeys,* 12th September, 1842.

goyles from old St. Giles', which they were then re-
storing, and disposed them on the gables and over the
door and about the garden; and the quarry which had
supplied them with building material, they draped with
clematis and carpeted with beds of roses. In process
of time the trees grew higher, and gave shade to the
cottage, and the evergreens sprang up and turned the
dell into a thicket." [1]

Here for the next fourteen years the family spent a
large part of their summers in place of taking a furnished house at North Berwick or elsewhere.

Hither at all seasons Louis would often retire alone or
in the company of a friend; here he gained a knowledge
of the Pentlands only to be acquired by living among
them; here he saw something of the country folk, and
enriched his vocabulary of Lallan; here made the acquaintance of John Todd the shepherd, and Robert
Young the gardener, and the military beggarman who
had a taste for Keats. This was to him *ille terrarum
angulus* of *Underwoods;* on the hill above Swanston
there lies the tiny pool, overhung by a rock, where he
"loved to sit and make bad verses"; and to this spot
he asked his old nurse, four months before he finally
left England, "some day to climb Halkerside for me (I
am never likely to do it for myself), and sprinkle some
of the well water on the turf."

Here one winter-tide he read Dumas again. "I would
return in the early night from one of my patrols with
the shepherd: a friendly face would meet me in the door,
a friendly retriever scurry upstairs to fetch my slippers;
and I would sit down with the *Vicomte de Bragelonne*

---

[1] *Picturesque Notes on Edinburgh*, p. 76.

for a long, silent, solitary, lamplit evening by the fire.
. . . I would rise from my book and pull the blind
aside, and see the snow and the glittering hollies chequer
a Scottish garden, and the winter moonlight brighten
the white hills." [1]

Now he joined in various sports; at first he rode a
good deal, and was even known to follow the hounds.
At this time he skated, chiefly from Edinburgh, at Duddingston Loch. It was in these years that he was in
Glenogil, in Mr. Barrie's country, and there caught as
many as three dozen trout in one day, and forthwith
forswore fishing. [2] Now he made his first acquaintance
with canoes, which at this time were introduced by Mr.
Baxter on the Firth of Forth. Sir Walter Simpson, the
companion of the *Inland Voyage*, was another pioneer,
and owned a large double canoe that often carried Stevenson, who had no boat of his own. His more experienced friends had no high opinion of his skill, but he
occasionally joined them at Granton, and later at
Queensferry, and spent many an afternoon in the fresh
air of the Forth and the healthful employment of his
paddle.

Conventional persons and conventional entertainments never had any attraction for him, and from general society in Edinburgh he was not long in with-
drawing himself. There were exceptions of course;
for several years after 1871 he took part in the private
theatricals at Professor Fleeming Jenkin's house: at first
as prompter, and afterwards in some minor parts, for
he never was proficient as an actor. But mostly he
preferred to see his friends apart from general company,

[1] *Memories and Portraits*, p. 237.   [2] *Letters*, ii. 345.

and as for his clothes, of which a great deal has been said—he dressed to please himself. It would be impossible to record the varying phases in which a certain vanity, a need of economy, and a love of ease were combined. The top-hat and frock-coat of convention became him extremely ill, and were finally abandoned after 1878, when as Jenkin's secretary he adopted them in Paris only to be referred to by the hotel clerk as a gentleman who knew all about Mabille. The notorious "black shirt," which was his favourite wear, dated, I believe, from his engineering days, and was made of dark-blue flannel. It was only a little care that was needed in selecting for him appropriate garments, but it was just this trouble he never was willing to take.

His father's was ever a hospitable house, and Louis was there able to entertain his friends. He joined the University Conservative Club, an organisation for elections, and made his first speech at its dinner; he dined with his Academy class for several years; and—more important than any of these—he was elected to the "Speculative Society"—that "Spec." of which the fame has gone abroad in the world largely by means of his writings.

"It is a body of some antiquity, and has counted among its members Scott, Jeffrey, Horner, Benjamin Constant, Robert Emmet, and many a legal and local celebrity besides. By an accident, variously explained, it has its rooms in the very buildings of the University of Edinburgh: a hall, Turkey-carpeted, hung with pictures, looking, when lighted up with fire and candle, like some goodly dining-room, a passage-like library, walled with books in their wire cages; and a corridor with a fireplace, benches, a table, many prints of famous members, and a mural tablet to the virtues of a former secretary. Here a member can warm himself and loaf and read; here, in defiance of Senatus-consults, he can smoke." [1]

The Society is limited to thirty ordinary members, who acquire honorary privileges at the end of four years. Meetings are held once a week from November to March; first an essay is read and criticised, and then a motion is debated. The roll is called thrice on each of these evenings, and at each call every ordinary member is bound to be present; an elaborate system of procedure has grown up, fenced in with penalties and fines. Stevenson was elected a member on 16th February, 1869, and in the proceedings he took an increasing interest. During his first complete session he attended six, during the next eight, and during the third session thirteen out of nineteen meetings. And in 1873 he wrote to one of his fellow-members: " O, I do think the Spec. is about the best thing in Edinburgh." [2]

The records of the Society contain several entries of interest, even if we do not press too closely the opinions advanced by a student in the heat of debate or the exhilaration of paradox.

The scene in *Weir of Hermiston* where the son of the Lord Justice-Clerk moves the abolition of Capital Punishment appears to have been not wholly imaginary.

[1] *Memories and Portraits*, p. 127.

[2] I must take this opportunity of expressing my thanks to the Society for kindly allowing me to have the necessary extracts made from their records, and especially to Mr. J. R. N. Macphail for obtaining this permission and in giving up his time to the task.

On March 1, 1870, Stevenson himself opened in the affirmative a debate on the question, "Is the Abolition of Capital Punishment desirable?" Like his hero, he found no seconder; but if he ever held the opinion, it certainly found no favour with him in after-life. The first essay he read before the Society (March 8, 1870) was on "The Influence of the Covenanting Persecution on the Scotch Mind," showing how closely this part of the national history occupied his attention. His opinion of the literature of the day was not high; in 1870 he moved that the revival of letters which took place early in the century is on the wane, and two years later he supported the view that American literature could compare favourably with the contemporaneous literature of England.

The "Spec." was probably the first place where Stevenson came into contact and rivalry with contemporaries who, being his equals, were not necessarily the friends of his own choice; and upon the members in general he seems to have made small impression. He was elected one of the five Presidents of the Society in 1872, but was at the bottom of the list and had only seven votes, whereas the first received eighteen, and the man next above him had thirteen supporters. In 1873 he was re-elected apparently without a contest; in his valedictory address, delivered in the same year, there is an amusing picture of the members, ending with a sketch of himself:—"Mr. Stevenson engaged in explaining to the other members that he is the cleverest person of his age and weight between this and California."

"It is good for boys to be violent and unruly, and to hate all constituted authority," he wrote before he himself had yet ceased to be a student, "for it is of such boys that good citizens are made." And in 1870 he himself, as a riotous student, fell into the hands of the police. He must have chafed at his own inaction and the injustice of the arrest, for, on that occasion at any rate, he was but a looker-on at one of the traditional snowball fights between the University and the Town. The magistrates, however, behaved with great discretion, inflicted lenient sentences, and merely bound Stevenson over to keep the peace.

But while the external course of his life seemed smooth, the deeper current had far more troubled a stream. For one thing, as we have seen, he was not interested in engineering, and all the time he could spare from it was given up to the pursuit which had taken firm possession of him. The art of writing was his one concern, and to learn this he was giving all his real self. In later life, when a master of his craft, he sometimes doubted whether he would not have preferred a life of action, had that been possible to him. But it was not for any reason of health that he gave up engineering, but because his impulse to letters was at this time overpowering, and admitted of neither substitute nor rival.

There were, however, besides the misspending of his time and the misdirection of his labour, other difficulties that were far more grave. He had begun to work out for himself his own views of life: his religion and his ethics, his relations to society and his own place in the universe. He was following out the needs of his mind and nature: strictly sincere with himself, he could never see things in their merely conventional aspect. He was "young in youth," and travelling at the fiery pace of his age and temperament; his senses were importunate, his intellect inquiring, and he must either find his own way, or, as he well might have done, lose it altogether.

When a young man with all the impetuosity of youth is involved in doubts as to the truth of religion, the constitution of society, and the contending claims of different duties, and further is bound to the service of a profession to which he is indifferent, while eagerly yearning after the practice of an art absorbing his whole powers, it is at once impossible he should be happy, and highly improbable that he should satisfy his parents.

Of all Stevenson's difficulties those concerned with religion were the most important, if for no other reason than that they alone affected his relations with his father. The one was questioning dogmas and observances which the other regarded it as impious to examine; and no sacrifice was too great for the father, no duty too arduous, if it could only avert from his child the doom of the freethinker. On the other hand, sooner than be tied to the doctrines of Calvinism, the lad called himself an atheist—such is ever the youthful formula of independence. Of the precise nature of his difficulties at this time he has left no record. He was revolting generally against doctrines held with severity and intolerance, and struggling for that wider view and larger conception of life, which he afterwards found to be less incompatible than he thought with the lessons of his earliest years.

He speaks of the startling effect that the Gospel of

St. Matthew produced on him,[1] but this seems to have been chiefly upon the social side. He was never at any time prone to compromise, and the discrepancy between Christ's teaching and the practice of Christian societies he was neither ready to explain away nor able to ignore.[2] As in religion he designated himself for the moment an atheist, so he seems in economics, if not in politics, to have become "a red-hot Socialist."[3] The direction of his views was no doubt partly due to the "healthy democratic atmosphere" of the Scottish University system.

"At an early age the Scottish lad begins his . . . experience of crowded class-rooms, of a gaunt quadrangle, of a bell hourly booming over the traffic of the city to recall him from the public-house where he has been lunching, or the streets where he has been wandering fancy-free. His college life has little of restraint, and nothing of necessary gentility. He will find no quiet clique of the exclusive, studious, and cultured; no rotten borough of the arts. All classes rub shoulders on the greasy benches. The raffish young gentleman in gloves must measure his scholarship with the plain, clever, clownish laddie from the parish school."[4]

But to him especially, the truant and the scapegrace,

---

[1] *Juvenilia*, p. 327. *Later Essays*, p. 278.

[2] At the "Spec.," on 12th November, 1872, he read an essay on "Two Questions on the Relations between Christ's Teaching and Modern Christianity." But on 24th November, 1871, he spoke against Communism being a maintainable theory. In March, 1871, he voted a want of confidence in Mr. Gladstone's Ministry, and probably throughout his life would, if compelled to vote, have always supported the Conservative candidate.

[3] *Virginibus Puerisque*, p. 64.

[4] "The Foreigner at Home," *Memories and Portraits*, p. 95.

the contrast came home with severity. In *Lay Morals* he unfolds some of the details of his experience in recounting " a few pages out of a young man's life."

" He was a friend of mine; a young man like others; generous, flighty, as variable as youth itself, but always with some high motions, and on the search for higher thoughts of life. . . . But he got hold of some unsettling works, the New Testament among others, and this loosened his views of life and led him into many perplexities. As he was the son of a man in a certain position, and well off, my friend had enjoyed from the first the advantages of education, nay, he had been kept alive through a sickly childhood by constant watchfulness, comforts, and change of air, for all of which he was indebted to his father's wealth.

" At college he met other lads more diligent than himself, who followed the plough in summer-time to pay their fees in winter; and this inequality struck him with some force. He was at that age of a conversible temper, and insatiably curious in the aspects of life; and he spent much of his time scraping acquaintance with all classes of man- and woman-kind. In this way he came upon many depressed ambitions and intelligences stunted for want of opportunity; and this also struck him. He began to perceive that life was a handicap upon strange, wrong-sided principles; and not, as he had been told, a fair and equal race. He began to tremble that he himself had been unjustly favoured, when he saw all the avenues of wealth, and power, and comfort closed against so many of his competitors and equals, and held unwearyingly open before so idle, desultory, and so dissolute a being as himself. . . .

97

My friend was only unsettled and discouraged, and filled full with that trumpeting anger with which young men regard injustices in the first blush of youth; although in a few years they will tamely acquiesce in their existence, and knowingly profit by their complications. Yet all this while he suffered many indignant pangs. And once when he put on his boots, like any other unripe donkey, to run away from home, it was his best consolation that he was now, at a single plunge, to free himself from the responsibility of this wealth that was not his, and to do battle equally against his fellows in the warfare of life."

Unfortunately the well-meant action of his parents added to his unhappiness a touch of squalor. They were generosity itself; they provided for their son all that they thought a young man could possibly want. So long as he cared for such entertainments, they gave dinners and dances to his friends, whom they welcomed (if thought suitable) on all occasions to their house; for his health and education there was nothing they were not ready to do. One thing only was wanting to him, and that was liberty, or rather the means of using it. They knew how generous he was by nature, probably they guessed how open-handed he was likely to be, and until he was three-and-twenty they restricted him —as others of his friends also were restricted—to half-a-crown or, at the most, five shillings a week as pocket-money. The result was that the lad went his own way, and frequented places which consorted with his means. This may have extended the future novelist's knowledge of man and woman and of the many aspects of human life, but it was scarcely a successful policy in his father's

eyes (had he but known) which placed his son's head-
quarters at a tobacconist's shop,[1] and sent him to the
Lothian Road and a succession of such hostelries as
"The Green Elephant," "The Twinkling Eye," and
"The Gay Japanee."

Stevenson's own account of it ran thus:—

"I was always kept poor in my youth, to my great
indignation at the time, but since then with my complete approval. Twelve pounds a year was my allowance up to twenty-three [which was indeed far too
little],[2] and though I amplified it by a very consistent
embezzlement from my mother, I never had enough
to be lavish. My monthly pound was usually spent
before the evening of the day on which I received it;
as often as not, it was forestalled; and for the rest of
the time I was in rare fortune if I had five shillings at
once in my possession. Hence my acquaintance was
of what would be called a very low order. Looking
back upon it, I am surprised at the courage with which
I first ventured alone into the societies in which I moved;
I was the companion of seamen, chimney-sweeps, and
thieves; my circle was being continually changed by
the action of the police magistrate. I see now the little
sanded kitchen where Velvet Coat (for such was the
name I went by) has spent days together, generally in
silence and making sonnets in a penny version-book;
and rough as the material may appear, I do not believe
these days were among the least happy I have spent.

[1] "Although tobacco is an admirable sedative, the qualities necessary for retailing it are neither rare nor precious in themselves."—
"An Apology for Idlers," *Virginibus Puerisque*, p. 90.

[2] The words in brackets are added in pencil.

I was distinctly petted and respected; the women were most gentle and kind to me; I might have left all my money for a month, and they would have returned every farthing of it. Such indeed was my celebrity, that when the proprietor and his mistress came to inspect the establishment, I was invited to tea with them; and it is still a grisly thought to me, that I have since seen that mistress, then gorgeous in velvet and gold chains, an old, toothless, ragged woman, with hardly voice enough to welcome me by my old name of Velvet Coat."

These were the days when there was most truth in the analogy that Stevenson loved to trace between himself and Robert Fergusson, the forerunner of Burns: the poor Edinburgh lad, who "died in his acute, painful youth, and left models of the great things that were to come": [1] "so clever a boy, so wild, of such a mixed strain, so unfortunate, born in the same town with me, and as I always felt, rather by express intimation than from evidence, so like myself." [2] So far indeed did he carry this sympathy that, in writing from Samoa, he expressed his conviction that in him Fergusson lived again. [3]

The days were the days of green-sickness, and they were often miserable. Many a time he leaned over the great bridge which connects the New Town with the Old, and watched the trains smoking out from under him, and vanishing into the tunnel on a voyage to brighter skies. [4] Often he haunted the station itself, envying the passengers; and again, "in the hot fits of

[1] *Letters*, ii. 223. [2] *Ibid.*, ii. 329. [3] *Ibid.*, ii. 223.
[4] *Picturesque Notes*, p. 4.

youth," he went to the Calton burying-ground, "to be unhappy." "Poor soul," he says of himself, "I remember how much he was cast down at times, and how life (which had not yet begun) seemed already at an end, and hope quite dead, and misfortune and dishonour, like physical presences, dogging him as he went."

Yet the days were the days of youth, and often they were days of happiness. The clouds rolled away in their season; most of the troubles were subjective, and though they were acutely felt, yet their ultimate solution was certain.

The one difficulty most immediately affecting his outer life—the pursuit of engineering—was, however, among the first to be solved. On April 8, 1871, Louis told his father of his extreme disinclination for the work, and asked to be allowed to follow literature. It must have come as a heavy disappointment to Thomas Stevenson, who, as we have seen, was devoted to the practice of his calling. Moreover, only twelve days previously Louis had read before the Royal Scottish Society of Arts his first and only contribution to the literature of his profession, a paper on a New Form of Intermittent Light, which was afterwards judged "well worthy of the favourable consideration of the Society, and highly creditable to so young an author."[1] The father felt the blow, but he must to some extent have been prepared for it by his son's entire lack of interest

[1] The proposed light has never been constructed in consequence of several mechanical difficulties, as I am informed by Mr. D. A. Stevenson, the present head of the firm and Engineer to the Commissioners of Northern Lighthouses.

in the solution of problems which to him were the most entrancing in the world. He seems to have met the request with calm; his wife's diary records that he was "wonderfully resigned"; and the matter was compromised without difficulty or delay. Engineering was to be given up forthwith, but lest Louis should find himself with no other profession than that of "failed author," he was to read Law and to be called to the Scottish Bar. If he chose to practise, he would have his profession; his necessary legal and historical studies would add more or less to his general culture, and he would be able during his preparation to carry on the literary training that was already occupying so large a portion of his time.

The general alleviation of his position was more gradual, but of this he has left an account, the fragment of a larger scheme of biography written in San Francisco in the beginning of 1880.[1]

"I had a happy afternoon scrambling with Bob upon the banks of the Water of Leith above Slateford. And so I may leave this part of my life and take it up in another direction. At last I am now done with morbidity and can wash my hands.

"BOOK III.—FROM JEST TO EARNEST

"I date my new departure from three circumstances: natural growth, the coming of friends, and the study of Walt Whitman. The order or degree of their effec-

[1] For Book I., *vide* p. 53 n. Of Book II. only the last lines survive, and the fragment on p. 99.

tiveness I shall not seek to distinguish. But I shall first say something of my friends.

" My cousin Bob,[1] who had now, after a long absence, returned to Edinburgh, is the man likest and most unlike to me that I have ever met. Our likeness was one of tastes and passions, and, for many years at least, it amounted in these particulars to an identity. He had the most indefatigable, feverish mind I have ever known; he had acquired a smattering of almost every knowledge and art; he would surprise you by his playing, his painting, his writing, his criticism, his knowledge of philosophy, and, above all, by a sort of vague, disconnected, and totally inexplicable erudition. What was specially his, and genuine, was his faculty for turning over a subject in a conversation.[2] There was an insane lucidity in his conclusions; a singular, humorous eloquence in his language, and a power of method, bringing the whole of life into the focus of the subject under hand; none of which I have ever heard equalled or even approached by any other talker. I am sure that he and I together have, in a brief, conspectory manner, turned over the stuff of a year's reading in one half-hour of talk. He was the most valuable man to talk to, above all in his younger days; for he twisted like a serpent, changed like the patterns in a kaleidoscope, transmigrated (it is the only word) from one point of view to another with a swiftness and completeness that left a stupid and merely logical mind panting in the rear; and so, in an incredibly brief space of time, helped you to view a question upon every side. In sheer

[1] The late R. A. M. Stevenson; *vide* p. 104 n.
[2] Cf. " Talk and Talkers," *Memories and Portraits*, p. 187.

trenchancy of mind, I have ever been his humble and distant follower. The multiplicity and swiftness of his apprehensions, if they do not bewilder, at least paralyse his mind. He is utterly without measure. He will spend a week in regulating the expenses of an imaginary navy; and then in ten minutes crush a subtle fallacy or create a new vein of criticism. We have perhaps only one moral quality in common: a desire to do justice to those with whom we are at enmity. I am now in my thirtieth year, and I have found sufficient excuses for all whom I think to have injured me but two; and for one of these I still hope to do the like. As for the other, I give him up to obscene furies; duck him where Stinchar[1] flows; it was he who first taught me, in my twenty-seventh year, to believe that it was possible for man to be evil with premeditation; and that was perhaps an evil enough service in itself.[2] But in this particular Bob so far outstrips or (may I say?) outshines me, that I have sometimes been put to the blush by the largeness and freedom of his allowances for others.[3]

[1] A river in Ayrshire, at the mouth of which is Ballantrae. Cf. Burns's song: " Behind yon hills where Stinchar flows."

[2] Cf. *Memoir of Fleeming Jenkin*, p. 151.

[3] Robert Alan Mowbray Stevenson was born in Edinburgh, 25th March, 1847, and died 18th April, 1900. He was educated at Windermere College and at Sidney Sussex College, Cambridge. He then studied painting chiefly at Antwerp and in France, but became an art critic about 1885, and from 1885 to 1889 was Professor of Fine Arts at University College, Liverpool. "The Art of Velasquez" and the monograph on Rubens in the *Portfolio* series are the chief works he has left behind him, but, like Gerard de Nerval, " il a versé plus d'une urne dans le tonneau sans fond du journalisme." These notes and the

" The next friend who came to me (I take them in the order of time) was, I think, Charles Baxter. I cannot characterise a personality so unusual in the little space that I can here afford. I have never known one of so mingled a strain. As a companion, when in spirits, he stands without an equal in my experience. He is the only man I ever heard of who could give and take in conversation with the wit and polish of style that we find in Congreve's comedies.[1] He is likewise the only person I ever knew who could *advise*, or, to explain more perfectly my meaning, who could both make

subsequent essay in *Memories and Portraits* give some idea of his talk as it was at this time — perhaps the most brilliant in England. In the *Pall Mall Magazine* for July, 1900, Mr. Henley describes its mellowing, and says of such copiousness and intolerance as ever distinguished "Spring-Heel'd Jack " : " 'T is a good ten years since I saw the last of that exorbitant and amazing person — a person, be it noted, ever, for all his amazingness and for all his exorbitancy — ever, I may insist, an influence for the best, alike in morals and in art; and I can say with a certain assurance that the younger men knew nothing of him. What they got in his room was a some one, bright-eyed, a little flushed, ever courteous, ever kindly, ever humorous, taking any bit of the universe as his theme, descanting upon it as if he had a prescriptive right in it, and delighting every one who listened by the unfailing excellence, wisdom, sanity (however insane it seemed at times) of what he had to say." And another of his friends, writing in the *Saturday Review* (28th April, 1900), says: " We know what the joy was of the 'Mermaid' since we have known him."

Of these earlier days he wrote to Louis as long ago as 1874: " We used to think we were like no one else about certain things, but that was a real phase too."

[1] He was, even then, as a letter from R. L. S. in 1894 reminds him, " a great maker of reminiscences," and to his influence, perhaps, it was partly due that Stevenson turned so early and so frequently to the past.

helpful suggestions and at the same time hold his tongue when he had none to offer.

"The next was James Walter Ferrier. It is only now when I come to describe them that I perceive how strange a crew were my associates; but Ferrier's strangeness was of a tragic character. The grandson of old Wilson, the son of Ferrier the metaphysician, he was gifted with very considerable abilities; he was by nature the most complete and gentle gentleman (I must risk the pleonasm) I have known.

"I never knew any man so superior to himself. The best of him only came as a vision, like Corsica from the Corniche. He never gave his measure either morally or intellectually. The curse was on him. Even his friends did not know him but by fits. I have passed hours with him when he was so wise, good, and sweet, that I never knew the like of it in any other.[1]

"The fourth of these friends was Sir Walter Simpson, son of Sir James who gave chloroform to the world. He was, I think, the eldest of my associates; yet he must have been of a more deliberate growth, for when we encountered, I believe we were about equal in intellectual development. His was a slow fighting mind. You would see him, at times, wrestle for a minute at a time with a refractory jest, and perhaps fail to throw

[1] I have here substituted a portion of a letter which Stevenson wrote upon hearing of the death of Ferrier (*Letters*, i. 281) for the original MS., which says nearly the same things in a more halting fashion, and is generally less suitable for quotation. For the finished study, pitched in a loftier key, the reader is referred to "Old Mortality" in *Memories and Portraits*.

it at the end. I think his special character was a profound shyness, a shyness which was not so much exhibited in society as it ruled in his own dealings with
himself. He was shy of his own virtues and talents,
and above all of the former. He was even ashamed of
his own sincere desire to do the right. More than half
the man, as you first knew him, was a humbug; and
that was utterly the worser part. But this very foible
served to keep clean and wholesome the unusual intimacy which united him, Baxter, and myself; for he
would permit no protestations and scarce any civility
between us. It is odd that this had to be dropped in
time; for, as we went on in life and became more seriously involved, we found it then more necessary to be
kind. Then, indeed, Simpson could show himself not
only kind but full of exceptional delicacies. Some of
them I did not appreciate till years after they were done
and perhaps forgotten by him. I have said his mind
was slow, and in this he was an opposite and perhaps
an antidote to Bob. I have known him battle a question
sometimes with himself, sometimes with me, month
after month for years; he had an honest stubborn-
ness in thinking, and would neither let himself be beat
nor cry victory.

"The mere return of Bob changed at once and for
ever the course of my life; I can give you an idea of
my relief only by saying that I was at last able to breathe.
The miserable isolation in which I had languished was
no more in season, and I began to be happy.[1] To have

[1] At this point it may be as well to mention the L. J. R., "that
mysterious society." It consisted of six members, and its meetings, of
which only five took place, were held at a public-house situated, I be-

no one to whom you can speak your thoughts is but a
slight trial; for a month or two at a time, I can support
it almost without regret; but to be young, to be daily
making fresh discoveries and fabricating new theories
of life, to be full of flimsy, whimsical, overpowering
humours, that seem to leave you no alternative but to
confide them or to die, and not only not to have, but
never to have had a confidant, is an astounding misery.
I now understand it best by recognising my delight
when that period was ended. I thought I minded for
nothing when I had found my Faithful; my heart was
like a bird's; I was done with the sullens for good;
there was an end of green-sickness for my life as soon
as I had got a friend to laugh with. Laughter was at
that time our principal affair, and I doubt if we could
have had a better. It is true we debated many things
from the first, above all, problems of art, in which we
advanced wonderfully; and it is also true that under all
this mirth-making there kept growing up and strength-
ening a serious, angry, and at length a downright hos-
tile criticism of the life around us. This time we call,
in looking back, the period of Jink.

"Jink was a word of our own; for we had a language, compounded of many slangs and languages, in
which we expressed, indifferently, common things that
had already a much better name in English, and the

lieve, in Advocates' Close, which had apparently been visited by
Burns. Its complete name was concealed with a mystery as deep and
not less important than that which broods over the Greek-letter societies of American colleges. Its principles, generally speaking, were
liberty of thought and freedom from prejudice. The abolition of the
House of Lords was, it is said, one of its tenets.

new or half-understood ideas for which there were no names, or none with which we were acquainted.

"As a rule of conduct, Jink consisted in doing the most absurd acts for the sake of their absurdity and the consequent laughter. I will give an instance of the colossal jests which we used to enact, and of which this at least is to be said, that if they were silly, they were never cruel. One of us was once travelling from Wales to Edinburgh, strangely dilapidated as usual in the matter of coin; and when he got to Crewe, he was stopped before the booking-office for a paltry half-crown. There were fifteen minutes to spare before the train started. He opened his portmanteau on the platform, got out a pair of dress-trousers, ran into the town, stumbled straight on a pawnbroker's shop, got his half-crown, and was back in time to book and get a seat. But when the hurry was over he began to wonder over a circumstance in this little comedy. When asked his name by the pawnbroker, he had replied instantly and without conscious thought, 'John Libbel,' and when further questioned as to the spelling, had rapped out in the same swift and perfectly mechanical way, 'Two B's.' On his return the matter was discussed. It seemed to us, I remember, a case of plenary inspiration; and we agreed, at last, that it must have been so, because the name was so suitable for one who pawned. It seemed to us, and it seems to me still, a mean, hungry, slinking sort of name; hence we thought that all of us should use it as a name to pawn under; and hence germinated the great idea of Libbelism. A large, growing, pushing society of men should go all over the world and continually pawn articles under the name of John Libbel; until at length, when some great German statist took it into his blockhead to examine the books of pawnbrokers, it would gradually dawn upon him that, in all lands and for year after year, innumerable persons all answering to this one name of John Libbel were daily engaged in the act of pawning, and yet when he turned his eyes outward on the world to follow the conduct of these persons in a different sphere, behold there would be no John Libbel, no, not one. We exulted over the mystification of the German statist. To pawn anything under this name was to perform an 'act of Libbelism.'

"I remember these words from the 'Corpus totius Juris Libbelismi,' which I drew up: 'vel si rem suam, vel si rem alienam, maxime quidem si rem alienam.'

"But the idea did not rest here: we had tasted blood, and soon began to find out other ways of building up evidence of this imaginary person's existence. We bought some type for marking pocket-handkerchiefs one day at the corner of North College Street, and retiring to a public-house, printed off, with incredible patience, many hundred visiting-cards with the name of 'Mr. Libbel.' The type being worthless, and the printing being done without a press, and amateur at that, you may conceive the aspect of the cards. These began to be handed about Edinburgh at a great rate, sometimes with manuscript additions which did not tend to improve the moral character of Mr. Libbel. A whole street would suddenly be flooded from end to end with Mr. Libbel's visiting-cards; or one would be softly pressed into the hand of a gentleman going by. Parcels, containing nothing, 'With Mr. Libbel's compliments,' were handed into houses. Letters from Mr. Libbel to leading citizens were carried by the unconscious postman. I have spent whole days going from lodging-house to lodging-house inquiring anxiously, 'If Mr. Libbel had come yet?' and when the servant or a landlady had told us 'No,' assuring her that he would come soon, and leaving a mysterious message. And at last—crowning point of the edifice—there came the Libbel Succession. Wherever we went, we had a notebook in our hand; we would put questions, look at each other, purse our lips, and gradually let it escape to our auditor, as if by accident, that we were agents looking for the heir to the great Libbel fortune. We tried to get an advertisement into the *Scotsman* newspaper, but the clerk plainly smelling a hoax, we were ejected from the office. Did we labour in vain from first to last? After all this apostledom, was there not one disciple? Did no two of our victims ever take counsel together, and after comparing notes, cry out: 'But who the devil is this Libbel?' We can never know now; but we were disinterested, we required none of the encouragement of success, we pursued our joke, our mystification, our *blague* for its own sake, and had a good time.

"Yet for this and other mad pranks of a like order, we were rewarded in a strange way, by one flash of infernal glory. This is so odd in itself that I must tell it with every particularity. One afternoon, hunting round for the absurd, we entered the shop of a jeweller called Bargany —— on —— Street, rather low down, and there proceeded for about quarter of an hour to pass off some piece of vaulting absurdity on the shopman. Suddenly the man's eye took fire, and he started back. 'I know who you are,' he cried; 'you 're the two Stevensons.' We were dumbfounded. 'Oh,' he went on, 'Bargany 's been dying to see you. He 'll be so vexed that he was out. Oh, *he* 's heard of your ongoings.' And the man shouted with laughter again and again. He told us to come back later in the afternoon, or any other afternoon, and have tea in the back shop with Bargany and his sister, who had also heard of us, and desired to make our acquaintance. And I must say if our reputation did us any justice, that sister was a liberal lady. Would you believe it? we never went back.

"To tell what else we did would be interminable and, besides, extremely tedious. As Bob said, we did nothing obvious; the least joke was spiced to us by being imbedded in mountains of monotony."

Here the manuscript breaks off. Some notes on an earlier page enable us to learn in what direction it might have been continued. "Whitman: humanity: L. J. R.: love of mankind: sense of inequality: justification of art: decline of religion: I take to the New Testament: change startling: growing desire for truth: Spencer: should have done better with the New Test."

Thus the coming of happiness was due partly to his friends and partly to his reading. To the list of the former there is still an addition to be made—the name of Fleeming Jenkin. It was in 1868 that Jenkin came to Edinburgh as Professor of Engineering, and it was first in the character of a truant that Stevenson came under his notice.[1] The professor was fifteen years older than his pupil—a difference in age which is often diffi-

[1] *Memoir of Fleeming Jenkin,* p. 155.

cult to surmount. But besides his boundless energy
and vitality, there was about Jenkin a perpetual boyish-
ness, which showed itself not least in this, that his development continued to the end of his life. His delight
in all that was high-minded and heroic, his fiery enthusiasm, his extraordinary readiness and spirit, were
just the qualities to win and to stimulate the younger
man. Moreover, at the time that Stevenson fell under
his influence, the detachment and independence of Jenkin's religious views rendered that influence of far
greater weight than if he had been content to yield a
lifeless assent to established observances and conventional creeds. Stevenson was in revolt, or meditating
an outbreak. Here was a man, ready to question everything, exercising a clear-sighted judgment, and yet full
of earnestness and piety, who " saw life very simple,"
who did not love refinements, but was "a friend to
much conformity in unessentials." And about Jenkin
there were these further points which distinguished him
from Stevenson's other friends, and gave him a great
advantage. He was the only one who had already
fought the battle of life, and not only was victorious
but knew how to carry his success.[1] Moreover, he
was the first of Stevenson's friends who was already
married. Perhaps the most charming passages in the
Memoir of Fleeming Jenkin are those which suggest
rather than describe the infinite tenderness and romance
which marriage brought into his life and made his house
all it was to those who loved him. And so to Stevenson it was from the first a double friendship, renewed
each spring in Edinburgh by the theatricals in which

[1] *Letters*, ii. 80.

he took part, and also by a long visit to the family in their country quarters. To Jenkin he resorted in many of his troubles, and from him and his wife he never failed to obtain the sympathy and wise counsel of which he stood in need. Mrs. Jenkin, writing in 1895, says that her husband loved him best of all his friends, and Stevenson, when he came to write Jenkin's biography, records what mingled pain and pleasure it was "to dig into the past of a dead friend, and find him, at every spadeful, shine brighter."[1]

Stevenson's numerous and characteristic letters to Jenkin were returned to their writer after his friend's death, and, in the confusion of the departure from Bournemouth, they were unfortunately destroyed. Of his first introduction to Mrs. Jenkin, she has herself given an account.

Late on a winter afternoon in 1868 she paid her first visit to 17 Heriot Row, and there found Mrs. Stevenson sitting by the firelight, apparently alone. They began to talk, when "suddenly, from out of a dark corner beyond the fireplace, came a voice, peculiar, vibrating; a boy's voice, I thought at first. 'Oh!' said Mrs. Stevenson, 'I forgot that my son was in the room. Let me introduce him to you.' The voice went on: I listened in perplexity and amazement. Who was this son who talked as Charles Lamb wrote? this young Heine with the Scottish accent? I stayed long, and when I came away the unseen converser came down with me to the front door to let me out. As he opened it, the light of the gas-lamp outside ('For we are very lucky, with a lamp before the door,' he sings) fell on him, and

[1] *Letters*, ii. 13.

I saw a slender, brown, long-haired lad, with great dark eyes, a brilliant smile, and a gentle, deprecating bend of the head. 'A boy of sixteen,' I said to myself. But he was eighteen, looking then, as he always did, younger than his age. I asked him to come and see us. He said, 'Shall I come to-morrow?' I said 'Yes,' and ran home. As I sat down to dinner I announced, 'I have made the acquaintance of a poet!' He came on the morrow, and from that day forward we saw him constantly. From that day forward too, our affection and our admiration for him, and our delight in his company, grew."

Thus much of his friends and their influence. There was also the other continual and stimulating influence of books, and though Stevenson was never a scholar in the strict and more arid sense, few men ever brought so great an enthusiasm to the studies of their choice. His ardour was now at its height. Twenty years later he wrote: "I have really enjoyed this book as I—almost as I—used to enjoy books when I was going twenty—twenty-three; and these are the years for reading." [1]

"Books were the proper remedy: books of vivid human import, forcing upon the minds of young men the issues, pleasures, busyness, importance, and immediacy of that life in which they stand; books of smiling or heroic temper, to excite or to console; books of a large design, shadowing the complexity of that game of consequences to which we all sit down, the hanger-back not least." [2]

Besides his books at home, he had always access to

[1] *Letters*, ii. 246.   [2] *Memories and Portraits*, p. 112.

the Advocates' Library, the great public library of Edinburgh, which is entitled to receive a copy of everything
published in the kingdom. But for the present the
question is of those works with which a man lives,
which for the time become an intimate part of himself,
and closer than any friend. Such were to Stevenson
the three already mentioned, the New Testament, Walt
Whitman,[1] and Herbert Spencer. Of the first he says
but little, and of that I have already spoken: to Whitman he has done a measure of justice in one of the
Familiar Studies, and also in a paper on " Books which
have Influenced Me."[2] In the latter, too, Mr. Herbert
Spencer also receives his meed of gratitude, and to him
succeed Shakespeare, Dumas, Bunyan, Montaigne, and

[1] " His book . . . should be in the hands of all parents and guar-
dians as a specific for the distressing malady of being seventeen years
old. Green-sickness yields to his treatment as to a charm of magic;
and the youth, after a short course of reading, ceases to carry the world
upon his shoulders " (p. 108).

[2] Republished in his *Later Essays*, in the Edinburgh Edition.

" I come next to Whitman's *Leaves of Grass*, a book of singular
service, a book which tumbled the world upside down for me, blew
into space a thousand cobwebs of genteel and ethical illusion, and
having thus shaken my tabernacle of lies, set me back again upon a
strong foundation of all the original and manly virtues.

" . . . Close upon the back of my discovery of Whitman, I came
under the influence of Herbert Spencer. No more persuasive Rabbi
exists, and few better. . . . His words, if dry, are always manly and
honest; there dwells in his pages a spirit of highly abstract joy, plucked
naked like an algebraic symbol, but still joyful; and the reader will
find there a *caput mortuum* of piety, with little indeed of its loveliness,
but with most of its essentials; and these two qualities make him a
wholesome, as his intellectual vigour makes him a bracing, writer. I
should be much of a hound if I lost my gratitude to Herbert Spencer."
— " Books which have Influenced Me," *Later Essays*, p. 279.

many others in rapid sequence, until the writer was manifestly overwhelmed in returning thanks to the whole world of books which brought him so much wisdom and happiness.[1]

But learning to write—there was the business of life. Although the description of the method by which he taught himself this most difficult of arts has been quoted again and again, and has long ago become classical, I have no alternative and no desire but to give it in this place. The process described had long begun when this period opened, as it continued after its close; but to these years it chiefly refers—a space of protracted and laborious application without encouragement or immediate reward.[2]

"All through my boyhood and youth I was known

[1] In a notebook of 1871-72 I find this *Catalogus Librorum Carissimorum:*—

Montaigne's *Essays*.	Hazlitt's *Table-Talk*.
Horace, his *Odes*.	Burns's works.
Pepys, his *Diary, esp. the Trip to Bristol, Bath, etc.*	*Tristram Shandy*.
	Heine.
Shakespeare, his works, *Lear, Hamlet, Falstaff, Twelfth Night*.	Keats.
	Fielding.

Scott, strange to say, does not appear, but though Stevenson now and again said hard things of Sir Walter, they were all upon the technical side, and his incomparable merits perhaps no one ever better understood. Not all books, however, were of service: elsewhere he bewails the inhumanity of *Obermann* (*Memories and Portraits*, p. 112) and counts *Moll Flanders* and *The Country Wife* more wholesome reading.

Compare also the beginning of "A Gossip on a Novel of Dumas's" and "The Ideal House," *Miscellanea*, p. 47.

[2] "A College Magazine," *Memories and Portraits*, p. 122.

and pointed out for the pattern of an idler; and yet I was always busy on my own private end, which was to learn to write. I kept always two books in my pocket, one to read, one to write in. As I walked, my mind was busy fitting what I saw with appropriate words; when I sat by the roadside, I would either read, or a pencil and a penny version-book would be in my hand, to note down the features of the scene or commemorate some halting stanzas. Thus I lived with words.

" And what I thus wrote was for no ulterior use; it was written consciously for practice. It was not so much that I wished to be an author (though I wished that too) as that I had vowed that I would learn to write. That was a proficiency that tempted me; and I practised to acquire it, as men learn to whittle, in a wager with myself. Description was the principal field of my exercise; for to any one with senses there is always something worth describing, and town and country are but one continuous subject. But I worked in other ways also; often accompanied my walks with dramatic dialogues, in which I played many parts; and often exercised myself in writing down conversations from memory.

" This was all excellent, no doubt; so were the diaries I sometimes tried to keep, but always and very speedily discarded, finding them a school of posturing and melancholy self-deception. And yet this was not the most efficient part of my training. Good though it was, it only taught me (so far as I have learned them at all) the lower and less intellectual elements of the art, the choice of the essential note and the right word: things that to

a happier constitution had perhaps come by nature.
And as regarded training, it had one grave defect; for
it set me no standard of achievement. So that there
was perhaps more profit, as there was certainly more
effort, in my secret labours at home. Whenever I read
a book or a passage that particularly pleased me, in
which a thing was said or an effect rendered with propriety, in which there was either some conspicuous
force or some happy distinction in the style, I must sit
down at once and set myself to ape that quality. I was
unsuccessful, and I knew it; and tried again, and was
again unsuccessful, and always unsuccessful; but at
least in these vain bouts I got some practice in rhythm,
in harmony, in construction and the co-ordination of
parts.

"I have thus played the sedulous ape to Hazlitt, to
Lamb, to Wordsworth, to Sir Thomas Browne, to Defoe, to Hawthorne, to Montaigne, to Baudelaire, and to
Obermann. I remember one of these monkey-tricks,
which was called 'The Vanity of Morals'; it was to
have had a second part 'The Vanity of Knowledge';
but the second part was never attempted, and the first
part was written (which is my reason for recalling it,
ghost-like, from its ashes) no less than three times:
first in the manner of Hazlitt, second in the manner of
Ruskin, who had cast on me a passing spell, and third
in a laborious pasticcio of Sir Thomas Browne. So
with my other works: *Cain,* an epic, was (save the
mark!) an imitation of *Sordello; Robin Hood,* a tale in
verse, took an eclectic middle course among the fields
of Keats, Chaucer, and Morris; in *Monmouth,* a tragedy,
I reclined on the bosom of Mr. Swinburne; in my in-

numerable gouty-footed lyrics, I followed many masters; in the first draft of *The King's Pardon*, a tragedy, I was on the trail of no less a man than John Webster; in the second draft of the same piece, with staggering versatility, I had shifted my allegiance to Congreve, and of course conceived my fable in a less serious vein—for it was not Congreve's verse, it was his exquisite prose, that I admired and sought to copy. . . . So I might go on for ever, through all my abortive novels, and down to my later plays, of which I think more tenderly, for they were not only conceived at first under the bracing influence of old Dumas, but have met with resurrections: one, strangely bettered by another hand, came on the stage itself and was played by bodily actors; the other, originally known as *Semiramis*, a tragedy,[1] I have observed on bookstalls under the alias of *Prince Otto*. But enough has been said to show by what arts of impersonation and in what purely ventriloquial efforts I first saw my words on paper.

"That, like it or not, is the way to learn to write; whether I have profited or not, that is the way. It was so Keats learned, and there was never a finer temperament for literature than Keats's. . . .

"It is the great point of these imitations that there still shines, beyond the student's reach, his inimitable model. Let him try as he please, he is still sure of failure; and it is an old and a very true saying that failure is the only highroad to success. I must have had some disposition to learn; for I clear-sightedly condemned my own performances. I liked doing them indeed; but when they were done, I could see they

[1] The tragedy was in blank verse, *Academy*, 19th May, 1900.

were rubbish. In consequence, I very rarely showed them even to my friends; and such friends as I chose to be my confidants I must have chosen well, for they had the friendliness to be quite plain with me. 'Padding,' said one. Another wrote: 'I cannot understand why you do lyrics so badly.' No more could I! Thrice I put myself in the way of a more authoritative rebuff, by sending a paper to a magazine. These were returned, and I was not surprised or even pained. If they had not been looked at, as (like all amateurs) I suspected was the case, there was no good in repeating the experiment; if they had been looked at—well then I had not yet learned to write, and I must keep on learning and living."

Thus the secret of learning was—for the right man —only the secret of taking pains: and yet in the history of his endeavours we find, where we should least expect it, a hereditary trait. It seems as absurd to couple with indolence the name of the indefatigable writer, as it was for him to bring his grandfather into a similar connection:[1] but it is from himself that we hear of this failing, although we know not to which year it must be referred.

"I remember a time when I was very idle, and lived and profited by that humour. I have no idea why I ceased to be so, yet I scarce believe I have the power to return to it; it is a change of age. I made consciously a thousand little efforts, but the determination from which these arose came to me while I slept and in the way of growth. I have had a thousand skirmishes to keep myself at work upon particular mornings,

[1] P. 5.

and sometimes the affair was hot; but of that great change of campaign, which decided all this part of my life and turned me from one whose business was to shirk into one whose business was to strive and persevere, it seems to me as though all that had been done by some one else. The life of Goethe affected me; so did that of Balzac; and some very noble remarks by the latter in a pretty bad book, the *Cousine Bette*. I daresay I could trace some other influences in the change. All I mean is, I was never conscious of a struggle, nor registered a vow, nor seemingly had anything personally to do with the matter. I came about like a well-handled ship. There stood at the wheel that unknown steersman whom we call God."[1]

This may be assigned to the time immediately before his retirement from engineering; but it might relate equally to several periods when he was unable to settle down to work: they were seldom of long duration, and, except before his own conscience, there was hardly any time when the author of the *Apology for Idlers* ever really neglected the tasks of his true vocation.

As to the products of his labours, editors, as he has told us, would have nothing to say to them. So he became an editor himself. Magazines had risen and fallen wherever the boy had gone; but none of his serials had yet attained the distinction of type. The idea of the *Edinburgh University Magazine* was started in the rooms of the "Spec." by four of the members of that society, of which Stevenson was the youngest and least esteemed; the history of its rise and fall (for print did not save it from the fate of its manuscript predecessors)

[1] *Reflections and Remarks on Human Life*, p. 40.

may be read in *Memories and Portraits*, while some of
Stevenson's contributions are to be found in the volume
of his *Juvenilia*.   Interesting as they are, they constitute
no great achievement, and the picture of "An Old Scots
Gardener," retouched in after-days, is the only piece
which has found a place with the works of his later
years.

"The magazine appeared in a yellow cover, which
was the best part of it, for at least it was unassuming;
. . . it ran four months in undisturbed obscurity, and
died without a gasp.   The first number was edited by
all four of us, with prodigious bustle; the second fell
principally into the hands of Ferrier and me; the third
I edited alone; and it has long been a solemn question
who it was that edited the fourth. . . .

"It was no news to me, but only the wholesome confirmation of my judgment, when the magazine strug-
gled into half-birth, and instantly sickened and subsided
into night. . . . I cleared the decks after this lost engagement; had the necessary interview with my father,
which passed off not amiss; paid over my share of expense; . . . and then, reviewing the whole episode, I
told myself that the time was not yet ripe, nor the man
ready; and to work again I went with my penny ver-
sion-books, having fallen back in one day from the
printed author to the manuscript student."[1]

To the list of the works—books, plays, and articles
—already mentioned, which were written at this time,
the following names may be added, as showing the
direction of his labours.   In 1868 he wrote *Voces Fi-
delium*, a series of dramatic monologues in verse; and

[1] *Memories and Portraits*, p. 132.

123

"the bulk of a Covenanting novel," possibly another attempt on Hackston of Rathillet or the Pentland Rising.[1] *The King's Pardon* (otherwise *Park Whitehead*) and *Edward Daven* likewise survive only as names; the manuscripts are gone, and we cannot even guess at the models on which they were planned; though the first of them seems to show that here, as well as in *Cain*, Robert Browning helped to educate the writer who of all others in his day perhaps the least resembled him in style.

A *Retrospect*, written at Dunoon in 1870, and the fragment of *Cockermouth and Keswick*, a visit to Cumberland in 1871, are printed in the Edinburgh Edition. The former contains the account of the spae-wife, "a poor, mad Highland woman," who—along with much nonsense—predicted that he was to visit America, was to be very happy, and was to be much upon the sea. In the latter is an admirable portrait, such as Thackeray would have loved, of the London theatrical manager, lording it in the inn smoking-room at Keswick. There were also written at this date the article on Colinton Manse, from which I have quoted so largely, and another similar paper on his solitary games, which was afterwards transformed into "Child's Play."[2]

In 1871 he wrote the paper on "A New Form of Intermittent Light for Lighthouses," which was highly praised, and received a £3 medal from the Royal Scottish Society of Arts, and in May, 1873, his paper "On the Thermal Influence of Forests" was communicated to the Royal Society of Edinburgh by his father, and duly

[1] *Memories and Portraits*, pp. 297, 305.
[2] *Memories and Portraits*.

appeared in the *Proceedings* of that Society. Both these are contained in the Edinburgh Edition, but whatever scientific value they possess, as literature they are undistinguishable from ordinary papers of the kind.

Meanwhile their author was reading for the Bar, or at any rate attending some of the necessary lectures in Civil Law, Public Law, and Political Economy. In the second of these subjects he was even third in the class and received honourable mention, and from Professor Hodgson he gained a certificate for essays.   .

During the years 1872 and 1873 he spent some months in the office of Messrs. Skene, Edwards & Bilton, Writers to the Signet, in order to learn conveyancing. Part of the process consisted in copying documents, and for this in Scotland it was customary to pay the pupil. Scott in this way increased his meagre pocket-money, probably to a far greater amount than Stevenson ever achieved. I find, nevertheless, that in July, 1873, the latter was paid six pounds as "about the amount of your writings during the period you have been in the office." The senior partner of this firm was the well-known historian and antiquary, Mr. W. F. Skene, the author of *Celtic Scotland*, but it seems that he was hardly at all brought into connection with his pupil, and that, in later years, either learned the other's quality with much regret for a neglected opportunity.

In November, 1872, Stevenson, having no degree or qualification for exemption, passed the preliminary examination for the Scottish Bar; the circumstances are worth mention only for the light they throw on his character and his education. French was one of the subjects offered, and only the day before the examination he discovered that questions would be set him in the grammar of that language. He forthwith procured a book and realised that here was a body of knowledge the very existence of which had been unknown to him. It was manifestly useless to attempt to get it up in four-and-twenty hours, so he went in, relying on his practical acquaintance with the idiom. His ignorance was exposed, but his knowledge and his plausibility induced and enabled the examiner "to find a form of words," and his French was accepted as adequate. Another subject was Ethical and Metaphysical Philosophy, and Hamilton or Mackintosh (it is undesirable to be too precise) was the book prescribed. I give Stevenson's own account of what took place, as I have heard him tell the story. "The examiner asked me a question, and I had to say to him, 'I beg your pardon, but I do not understand your phraseology.' 'It's the text-book,' he said. 'Yes; but you couldn't possibly expect me to read so poor a book as that.' He laughed like a hunchback, and then put the question in another form; I had been reading Mayne, and answered him by the historical method. They were probably the most curious answers ever given in the subject; I don't know what he thought of them, but they got me through."

In 1872 he proposed to take a summer session at some German university with Sir Walter Simpson, who was also studying Law. But his mother grew so nervous that he gave up the scheme, and in place of it the friends spent two or three weeks together during the first part of August, chiefly in lodgings in Frankfurt. His parents joined him at Baden-Baden, and he then went for a short walking tour in the Black Forest.

This was the single occasion on which he crossed the Channel during this period of his life, and indeed in these years he was hardly out of Scotland but for his trip to the Lakes, and a visit to R. A. M. Stevenson at Cambridge, where he had a glimpse of the life of the English undergraduate. The last twelve months are of interest as the only time when he turned his attention at all seriously to the study of the German language and literature. For the next year or two there is an occasional reference to Heine or Goethe in his letters, and even a few quotations, chiefly in his unpublished fragments. But with these insignificant exceptions German appears to have passed over him without effect, and French was the only modern language that ever exercised an influence upon his style.

But Stevenson as he was in the later years of this period may best be seen in the curiously diverse entries of a short diary kept on a folio sheet of paper upon his first entrance to the lawyers' office. I have printed nearly the whole of it for the sake of the contrasts; the high spirits and the sentiment, the humour, the humanity and the immaturity, make a remarkable conjunction. Already it would be difficult for any one to read it without either recognising the author, or else prognosticating for him a future which, at any rate, should be neither commonplace nor obscure.

" *Thursday, May 9th* [*1872*].[1]—Went to office for first time. Had to pass an old sailor and an idiot boy, who tried both to join company with me, lest I should be late for office. A fine sunny, breezy morning,

[1] The year is settled beyond question by the corresponding entries in his mother's diary.

walking in. A small boy (about ten) calling out 'Flory' to a dog was very pretty. There was a quaint little *tremolo* in his voice that gave it a *longing*, that was both laughable and touching. All the rest of the way in, his voice rang in my memory and made me very happy.

"*Friday, May 10th*.—Office work—copying, at least —is the easiest of labour. There is just enough mind-work necessary to keep you from thinking of anything else, so that one simply ceases to be a reasoning being and feels *stodged* and stupid about the head, a consummation devoutly to be wished for.

"*Sunday, May 21st* [*19th*].—My father and I walked over to Glencorse to church. A fat, ruddy farm wench showed us the way; for the church, although on the top of a hill, is so buried among the tree-tops that one does not see it till one trips against the plate.[1] It is a quaint old building, and the minister, Mr. Torrance (his father and grandfather were here before him), is still more quaint and striking. He is about eighty; and he lamed himself last summer dancing a reel at a wedding. He wears black thread gloves; and the whole manner of the man in the pulpit breathes of last century.

"*Monday, May 12th* (*20th*).—In all day at the office. In the evening dined with Bob. Met X——, who was quite drunk and spent nigh an hour in describing his wife's last hours—an infliction which he hired us to support with sherry *ad lib*. Splendid moonlight night. Bob walked out to Fairmilehead with me. We were in a state of mind that only comes too seldom in a lifetime.

[1] *I.e.* the plate for contributions, which is left at the door of Scotch churches.

We danced and sang the whole way up the long hill,
without sensible fatigue. I think there was no actual
conversation—at least none has remained in my memory: I recollect nothing but ' profuse bursts of unpre-
meditated song.' Such a night was worth gold untold.
Ave pia testa! After we parted company at the toll, I
walked on counting my money, and I noticed that the
moon shone upon each individual shilling as I dropped
it from one hand to the other; which made me think
of that splendid passage in Keats, winding up with the
joke about the ' poor patient oyster.' [1]

" *Wednesday, 22nd.* — At work all day at Court—work
being periphrasis for sitting still, taking three luncheons,
and running two errands. In the evening started
in the rain alone, and seeing a fellow in front, I whis-
tled him to wait till I came up. He proved to be a pit-
worker from Mid-Calder, and—*faute de mieux*—I bribed
him by the promise of ale to keep me company as far
as New Pentland Inn. . . . I heard from him that the
Internationale was already on foot at Mid-Calder, but
was not making much progress. I acquitted myself as
became a child of the *Proprietariat*, and warned him,
quite apostolically, against all conversation with this
Abomination of Desolation. He seemed much impressed, and more wearied.

" He told me some curious stories of body-snatching
from the lonely little burying-ground at Old Pentland,
and spoke with the exaggerated horror that I have always observed in common people of this very excusa-
ble misdemeanour. I was very tired of my friend be-

[1] The references are to Shelley's *Skylark*, l. 5; Horace, *Odes*, iii.
21, 4; Keats's *Endymion*, iii. 67.

fore we got back again, and so I think he was of me. But I paid for the beer; so he had the best of it.

"*Friday, July 5th.*—A very hot sunny day. The Princes Street Gardens were full of girls and idle men, steeping themselves in the sunshine. A boy lay on the grass under a clump of gigantic hemlocks in flower, that looked quite tropical and gave the whole garden a southern smack that was intensely charming in my eyes. He was more ragged than one could conceive possible. It occurred to me that I might here play *le dieu des pauvres gens*, and repeat for him that pleasure that I so often try to acquire artificially for myself by hiding money in odd corners and hopelessly trying to forget where I have laid it; so I slipped a halfpenny into his ragged waistcoat pocket. One might write whole essays about his delight at finding it."

The most important event of the year for him sounds in itself one of the most trivial that can well be imagined —a visit to a country parsonage in Suffolk. A granddaughter of the old minister of Colinton had several years before married the Rev. Churchill Babington, Disney Professor of Archæology in the University of Cambridge, and formerly a Fellow of St. John's College, who had taken the college living of Cockfield, a few miles from Bury St. Edmunds. Here Stevenson had paid a visit in 1870, one of those excursions into England of which he speaks in the essay on " The Foreigner at Home," and from which he received "so vivid an impression of foreign travel and strange lands and manners." These sensations were now renewed and deepened, but the later visit was to have other and more lasting effects: Stevenson now met for the first time two fellow-guests, whose friendship became at once an important element in his life, affecting his development, changing his horizon, and opening for him a direct outlook into the world of letters in which he was to be hereafter so brilliant a figure. The first of these, a connection by marriage and intimate friend of his hostess, was the Mrs. Sitwell to whom those letters were addressed which throw so much light on the inner feelings and thoughts of the ensuing period of Stevenson's life. The second was Mr. Sidney Colvin, who then and there began that friendship which was so immediately helpful, which survived all shocks of time and change, which separation by half the world seemed only to render more close and assiduous, and which has its monument in the *Vailima Letters*, in the two volumes of Stevenson's other correspondence, and in the final presentation of his works. Mr. Colvin was then still resident at Cambridge as a Fellow of Trinity College, and had that same year been elected Slade Professor of Fine Arts in the University. Although Stevenson's elder by only a few years, he had already established for himself a reputation as a critic in literature and art, was favourably regarded by editors, and was fast becoming a personage of influence and authority.

It might seem that the list of Stevenson's friends already included as many as one man could retain in intimate relation; but for these two, and others yet to come, there was ample room. A few years after this he questions whether any one on this earth be so wealthy as to have a dozen friends, and indeed the doubt is permissible to most of us unless we knew Stevenson. Only six months before, in one of the morbid moods he was gradually putting behind him, as he sloughed the unhappiness of his youth, he had written down the chief desires of his heart. "First, good health: secondly, a small competence: and thirdly, O Du Lieber Gott! friends." Seldom was any prayer more fully answered than this last petition. Had he but known, the means of gaining it were already within his hands in a measure rarely granted to any man. At this very time, Mr. Colvin tells us,[1] "his social charm was already at its height." "He was passing through a period of neatness between two of Bohemian carelessness as to dress, and so its effect was immediate." But indeed at any time he "had only to speak in order to be recognised in the first minute for a witty

[1] *Letters*, i. 45, xxxix, xl.

and charming gentleman, and within the first five for a master spirit and man of genius."

At all events, by his hosts and by his fellow-guests his attraction was quickly felt, and the month of August, which passed away with no other episodes than a croquet party or a school feast, was nevertheless a landmark in his career.

From Suffolk he returned to Swanston with increased confidence and raised hopes, and at once plunged into work. The essay on "Roads" was completed and sent to the *Saturday Review*, and he began a paper on "Walt Whitman."[1]

But the preceding winter had tried him in mind and body, and he was now further weakened by a severe attack of diphtheria. In February his father had come across a draft of the constitution of the L. J. R. (p. 107, footnote), and had taken the society as seriously as the youngest of its members could have wished. The acute misunderstanding was limited to part of this year, and then by degrees it passed away. When Mr. Stevenson had determined beforehand on any course of action, he would throw himself into the part he had proposed with an energy and emphasis which were often, unconsciously to himself, far in excess of the situation or of the words he had intended to employ. "I have the family failing of taking strong views," he had written to his future wife in 1848, "and of express-

[1] It was this article that he afterwards described :—" I had written another paper full of gratitude for the help that had been given me in my life, full of enthusiasm for the intrinsic merit of the poems, and conceived in the noisiest extreme of youthful eloquence."—Preface to *Familiar Studies*.

ing those views strongly." A scene with him was no figure of words: he suffered the extreme of the emotions he depicted; and the knowledge and fear of this result made any difference between them very painful to his son. The differences arose, or threatened to arise again, the winter was coming on, and Louis' work came to an end.

An idea had arisen that he might be called not to the Scotch, but to the English Bar; and as his hopes were now directed towards London, the scheme was very welcome. To London accordingly he went in the last week of October with a view of entering one of the Inns of Court and passing the preliminary examination, if he could convince the examiners. The scheme was quickly laid aside. His friends in town found him so unwell that they at once insisted on his seeing Dr. (afterwards Sir Andrew) Clark. The diagnosis was plain — nervous exhaustion with a threatening of phthisis: the prescription was chiefly mental — a winter in the Riviera by himself, and in complete freedom from anxiety or worry. His mother came and saw him off, and on the 5th of November he started for Mentone, three weeks before his article on "Roads" had appeared in the *Portfolio*, of which P. G. Hamerton was editor.

How he sat in the sun and read George Sand his letters tell us; and all that he thought and felt and saw during the first six weeks was written down next spring in "Ordered South": a paper "not particularly well written," he thought, but "scrupulously correct." In the meantime, in "numbness of spirit" he rested and recovered strength. It was one of the halting-places of life, and there he sat by the wayside to recruit and prepare for a fresh advance. Mrs. Sitwell's letters brightened his solitude, as they had already cheered and helped him in Edinburgh. His answers to her show better than any analysis or description the solace and the strength which came to him from her hands. To over-come depression, to realise a due proportion in the troubles of youth, to surmount the passing moods of immaturity — all this falls more or less to the lot of every man. It is the good fortune of some to receive in this crisis that service which it is generally beyond the power of a man to bestow, and which is possible only for the few women who combine a quick intelli-gence and a knowledge of the world with charm of temperament and intuition heightened by sympathy.

In his hotel at Mentone Stevenson made the acquain-tance of two or three congenial people, who lent him Clough and other books which he read with interest; but as yet he was too weak for any serious reading, and was hardly fit for the exertion of talking to strangers. His internal struggles were of course not at an end, although he found them for the time less harass-ing. His moral doubts changed with his position, and took on a new phase. His own account, of which I have already quoted a part, after mentioning the circum-stances of his being sent abroad for his health, thus continues : —

"In the meantime you must hear how my friend acted. Like many invalids he supposed that he would die. Now should he die, he saw no means of repaying this huge loan which, by the hands of his father, man-kind had advanced him for his sickness. In that case it would be lost money. So he determined that the advance should be as small as possible; and, so long as he continued to doubt his recovery, lived in an upper room, and grudged himself all but necessaries. But so soon as he began to perceive a change for the better, he felt justified in spending more freely, to speed and brighten his return to health, and trusted in the future to lend a help to mankind, as mankind, out of its treasury, had lent a help to him."[1]

In April he described the course of his recovery to his mother in similar terms. "I just noticed last night a curious example of how I have changed since I have been a little better: I burn two candles every night now; for long, I never lit but one, and when my eyes were too weary to read any more, I put even that out and sat in the dark. Any prospect of recovery changed all that."

By the middle of December one stage of his convalescence was already made. He was now to experience another advantage of his newly-formed friendships, as Mr. Colvin joined him at Mentone, and supplied the intimate conversation and discussion which had become his chief need. There was no great change in his life; they passed the time quietly enough, together or apart, as the fancy took them; reading *Woodstock* aloud, or plunged in talk on any or all subjects; sitting in the olive yards or in a boat, basking in the sun; or in "some nook upon St. Martin's Cape, haunted by the voice of breakers, and fragrant with the threefold sweetness of the rosemary and the sea pines and the sea."

For a few days they went to Monte Carlo, where they "produced the effect of something unnatural upon the people," because where everybody gambled all night, they spent their evenings at home; but they soon returned to Mentone, and there in the hotel to which the chance of accommodation brought them, were fortunate in finding a small but very cosmopolitan society, which greatly brightened Stevenson's stay when his companion had to leave him. The chief members of this little coterie were a Georgian lady and her sister with two little daughters; M. Robinet, a French painter; and an American and his wife and child, "one of the best story-tellers in the world, a man who can make a whole table d'hôte listen to him for ten minutes while he tells how he lost his dog and found him again." With the younger of the Russian children, Nelitschka, "a little polyglot button" of only two and a half, who spoke six languages, or fragments of them, Stevenson at once struck up a great friendship, and his letters for the next three months are full of her, and her sayings and doings.

She was almost, if not quite, the only very young child who ever came much under his notice after the days of his own boyhood, and she seems to have been so extraordinarily brilliant and fascinating a little creature that there is nothing to wonder at in the great attraction which she had for him. The ladies, moreover, were women of cultivation and refinement; full of spirits, and always devising fresh amusements: telling fortunes, writing characters, dancing Russian dances and singing Russian airs, and charmed, to Stevenson's intense delight, by what he afterwards loved to call, with James Mohr, "the melancholy tunes of my native mountains." It was one of the episodes of real life; an introduction of characters who never reappear in the story, an episode such as literature rejects; but it made Stevenson's path smoother at a time when he was unable to climb steep places, and it took his thoughts off himself and hastened his recovery, while he was still unfit for prolonged exertion or any serious study.

Their circle was afterwards increased by the arrival of another friend of the Russians, the prince whose clever and voluble talk he has described in one of his letters, by whom he was nearly persuaded to take a course of Law, during the summer, at the University of Göttingen. In this time and place also began Stevenson's friendship with Mr. Andrew Lang, who was then staying in the Riviera and one day called upon Mr. Colvin. The impression Stevenson produced was, Mr. Lang confesses, "not wholly favourable": —

"A man of twenty-two, his smooth face, the more girlish by reason of his long hair, was hectic. Clad in a wide blue cloak, he looked nothing less than English, except Scotch." The impression received was that the other was "Oxfordish"; but Mr. Lang may console himself with the thought that this was before he had avowed his preference for St. Andrews. In spite of so tepid a beginning the acquaintance prospered, and grew into a friendship which endured until the end.

When Mr. Colvin, after one brief absence, finally returned to England, his companion was already working again, though still far from strong. Even by the middle of March, he says that he is "idle; but a man of eighty can't be too active, and that is my age."

As the days went on, it was time for him to turn northwards, but he was loth to go. He wrote to his mother: "*22nd Feb., 1874.*—What keeps me here is just precisely the said society. These people are so nice and kind and intelligent, and then as I shall never see them any more, I have a disagreeable feeling about making the move. With ordinary people in England, you have always the chance of rencountering one another; at least you may see their death in the papers; but for these people, they die for me and I die for them when we separate." On such terms he parted from them, not without the promise of a visit to their home in Poland, which, by no fault of his, was never accomplished.

In the beginning of April he reached Paris, and there found his cousin R. A. M. Stevenson, who had now taken up painting as a profession, and had been studying during the winter at Antwerp. This was Louis' first independent acquaintance with Paris, and he delayed his return to Edinburgh till the end of the month, when the weather in the North might be more favourable. But this was only a measure of caution, and for several years to come we hear no more of his health as affecting his movements, or seriously hindering his work.

On his return home he found that many of his troubles had vanished. He had not of course solved the riddle of the universe, nor adjusted all contending duties, nor mastered all his impulses and appetites. He had not learned to handle his pen with entire precision, or to say exactly the thing he wished in the manner perfectly befitting it; nor was his way of life open before him. But his relations with his parents were on the old footing once more, and in the religious question a *modus vivendi* seems to have been estab-

lished with his father. Probably nothing short of dog-
matic orthodoxy would have given entire satisfaction,
but at least this much already was gained, that the
son's character for honesty was established, and his
desire for the truth fully recognised.

The question of his allowance was now reconsidered.
The man who had been trusted freely with all the
money necessary for his expensive sojourn abroad
could not be put back to his small pocket-money, and
it was settled that in future he was to receive seven
pounds a month, more even than he himself had
thought of suggesting.

Money at his command and friends in the South
forthwith changed his mode of life. For the whole
seven years of the preceding period he had only crossed
the Border thrice, but henceforth he was never con-
tinuously at home for more than three months at a
time. Three springs and two autumns he spent in
Edinburgh or at Swanston, but in the intervals his face
became familiar in London, Paris, and the resorts of
painters near Fontainebleau. But all the time he never
went far afield, and between 1874 and 1879 seems not
to have travelled further than three hundred miles from
the English coast.

In Edinburgh his attention still had for some little
time to be given to the study and pursuit of the Law.
All idea of the English Bar was apparently given up,
and in the winter session of 1874 he resumed his at-
tendance at the lectures of the University professors on
Conveyancing, Scots Law, and Constitutional Law and
History. On July 14, 1875, he successfully passed his
Final Examination, and two days after was called to

the Scottish Bar. On the 25th he had his first compli-
mentary brief, and the following day he sailed for
London on his way to France. "Accept my hearty
congratulations on being done with it," Jenkin wrote.
"I believe that is the view you like to take of the beginning you have just made." Stevenson returned,
however, in the end of September, and during the
next few months made some sort of effort to practise,
although he does not seem to have impressed anybody
outside his own family as being a serious lawyer. He
frequented the great hall of the Parliament House,
which, like Westminster in old days, is the centre of
the courts, and the haunt of advocates waiting for
business. The brass plate with his name, usual in
Scotland, was affixed to the door of 17 Heriot Row,
and he had the fourth or fifth share in the services of a
clerk, whom it is alleged that he did not know by
sight. He had in all four briefs, and the total of his
fees never reached double figures. One piece of business might, he told me, have assumed real importance,
but a compromise brought it to an end. "If it had
prospered," he said, "I might have stuck to the Bar,
and then I suppose I should have been dead of the
climate long ago."

Once only was he conspicuously before the Court,
and this publicity was due neither to the weightiness
of the matter nor to the brilliancy of the advocate.
One day he met in the street a certain judge of the
Court of Session, whom he saluted in the customary
manner. Stevenson had just emerged from a public-
house, and was dressed at the time in a suit of old
clothes which may have been dear to his heart, but

were certainly not of the style habitual to members of the Bar. The judge looked surprised, but acknowledged the salute and passed on. When Stevenson reached home, he found a brief waiting for him with instructions to "revive "[1] a certain case the next day before this very judge. At the hour appointed he appeared in his robes, wigged and properly habited, and expecting the empty court usual for such formal business. But he reckoned without numbers of his friends, who, having got wind of the brief, came in to see how he would acquit himself, and the court was crowded. The judge scented a joke; recognised his young friend of the day before; asked who he was, and proceeded to require a great deal of entirely unnecessary information about the details of the case. The brief contained no allusion to these facts; counsel was completely ignorant of the history; the solicitor took care to keep well out of the way, and enjoyed the joke from the back of the court, until at last Stevenson's eye fell upon him, and the judge was referred to him for all further facts. So counsel escaped, but he had his quarter of an hour.

The Advocates' Library in the Parliament House is the best in Scotland; and here Stevenson hoped to get some of his literary work done, while he was waiting for briefs. But the division of interests and the attractive company of his fellows were too unsettling; he soon returned to his own upper room in his father's house, and came no more to the *Salle des Pas Perdus*.

But although, after he abandoned Parliament House,

[1] *I.e.* make a purely formal motion that it be replaced in the list, in order to prevent it from lapsing.

143

he was no longer confined to the city of his birth, it was still his home and the point of return from his wanderings in England or abroad. Three of the first four friends named in the preceding chapter were, like himself, now released from the necessity of living constantly in Edinburgh, yet their connection with it was maintained, and they continued more or less frequently to visit it; while Professor Jenkin and Mr. Baxter remained resident there as before.

Nor did Stevenson's manner of life, at the times when he was in Edinburgh, suffer any sudden change. We must think of him in Scotland at this time as living chiefly in the society of a few intimates, still wandering about the city and its neighbourhood, "scraping acquaintance with all classes of man- and woman-kind," travelling deliberately through his ages and getting the heart out of his own liberal education, still to some extent in bonds to himself, though he had escaped in a degree from circumstance. No longer as a supplement to professional studies, but now as his avowed business, he wrote and rewrote, he blotted and recast his essays, tales, verses, and plays as before, and accomplished much solid work. From general society he still held aloof, and it was in 1875 that he last took part in the Jenkins' theatricals, acting the Duke in *Twelfth Night*.

"He played no character on the stage as he could play himself among his friends," was his verdict upon Jenkin, and it was even more applicable to himself where his own friends were concerned; but as yet he could not modify his attitude towards the burgess or the Philistine, or forego the intolerance of youth.

All this did not heighten his popularity or the estimation in which he was held, nor was he generally looked upon at this time as likely ever to bring honour to his native city. The brilliance and diversity of his talk appealed to few of his fellow-citizens, whether old or young, and merely disconcerted those whose minds ran in narrower grooves. Mostly they perceived little more than the exterior of the lad with his dilapidated clothes, his long hair, and distaste for office life. The companions who knew him best did not spare their criticism or laughter, and it was at this time that names like Flibbertigibbet and Mr. Fastidious Brisk were aimed at his volubility and exaggeration on the one hand, and a supposed tendency to sprightliness and affectation of phrase upon the other.

It is a keen eye which can discern in a young man the difference between the belief in gifts which he does not possess, and his consciousness of powers as yet undeveloped, until Time, which tries all, reduces the one and justifies the other. It was chiefly the older men who looked with a kindly glance upon the manifestations of his youth, such as old Mr. Baxter, who had for him as warm an appreciation as his son Charles had found in turn at the hands of Thomas Stevenson; Mr. J. T. Mowbray, the family lawyer, a grim, dry, warm-hearted old bachelor, whom I have always fancied to be the original of Mr. Utterson in *Jekyll and Hyde;* Mr. Robert Hunter, of whom Stevenson has left a speaking portrait in the second part of " Talk and Talkers "; and other friendly veterans. These seem best to have realised the good that was in him, and indeed the husk is hardly noticeable to those who can read (as his contemporaries could not) how the frail lad found a lost child of three crying in the street in the middle of the night, and carried him half over Edinburgh, wrapped in his own greatcoat, while he sought in vain for the missing parents.[1]

And still, as in his childhood and as in most of his books, happiness came to him chiefly in the country. Long walks in the neighbourhood of Edinburgh; summer evenings in the garden at Swanston, or on Caerketton or Allermuir; days passed in canoeing on the Forth at Queensferry, or skating upon Duddingston Loch — these were the chief part of his outdoor life, and the last of his time that was spent amid the scenery of his boyish days.

In August, 1874, he was yachting for a month with Sir Walter Simpson and Mr. T. Barclay, on the west coast of Scotland — a happy experience not to be renewed for many a long year. The *Heron*, a fore-and-aft schooner of sixteen tons, had two Devon men as crew, and their labours were supplemented by the help of the owners and their friends. Stevenson lived a hard, open-air life, and throve upon it. "My health is a miracle. I expose myself to rain, and walk, and row, and over-eat myself. I eat, I drink, I bathe in the briny, I sleep." His return to Swanston was characteristically announced: "I left my pipe on board the yacht, my umbrella in the dog-cart, and my portmanteau by the way," and he reached home without his luggage, in a hat borrowed from one of his friends and a coat belonging to another.

In the following winter there came to him a new

[1] *Letters*, i. 89.

friendship. "Yesterday,[1] Leslie Stephen, who was down here to lecture, called on me and took me up to see a poor fellow, a poet who writes for him, and who has been eighteen months in our infirmary, and may be, for all I know, eighteen months more. It was very sad to see him there in a little room with two beds, and a couple of sick children in the other bed; a girl came in to visit the children, and played dominoes on the counterpane with them; the gas flared and crackled, the fire burned in a dull, economical way; Stephen and I sat on a couple of chairs, and the poor fellow sat up in his bed with his hair and beard all tangled, and talked as cheerfully as if he had been in a king's palace, or the great King's palace of the blue air."

Here was no ordinary patient: the poet was Mr. W. E. Henley, who had come to Edinburgh to be under the care of Lister. The cheerful talk was but the first of many; if we may treat Stevenson's essays[2] as autobiographical, for a part of his youth he was wont to "avoid the hospital doors, the pale faces, the sweet whiff of chloroform," but that time was now past. Here was a man of kindred spirit to himself, in need of the companionship that none could better give, and from that time forth Stevenson was his friend, and placed himself and all that he had at his disposal. He soon returned, bringing books, piles of Balzac, "big yellow books, quite impudently French,"[3] and with the books he brought Mr. Baxter and others of his friends.

[1] 13th February, 1875. *Letters*, i. 86.
[2] "Old Mortality," *Memories and Portraits*, p. 111.
[3] *Book of Verses*, p. 47, by William Ernest Henley.

In return, he found a friendship based on common tastes in literature and music, the talk of a true poet, the insight of one of the freshest and clearest and strongest of critics, whose training had been free from academic limitations, and whose influence was different in kind from the criticism on which the younger man had learned to rely, though not less full of stimulation and force.

In these years he first discovered that taste for classical music which was afterwards fostered by successive friends. The revelation dated from a concert in Edinburgh for which some one had given him a ticket, and to which he went with reluctance. It was a Beethoven quartet, I think, that then burst upon him for the first time, and on that day he permanently added another to the many pleasures he so keenly enjoyed, although it was some years before he attempted to make any music for himself.

To London in these years he paid frequent visits, and several times stayed with Mr. Colvin at Cambridge, besides spending a week or two with him at Hampstead in June, 1874. This last occasion, however, and a return to the same place in the autumn of that year were practically indistinguishable from his life in London. On June 3, 1874, after only six weeks' delay, he was elected a member of the Savile Club,[1] which had been founded five years before, and was still in its original house, 15 Savile Row. This was for the next five years the centre of his London life, and though it

[1] Mr. Colvin proposed him, and he was supported by Mr. Andrew Lang, Professor Fleeming Jenkin, Mr. Basil Champneys, Professor W. K. Clifford, and Mr. C. B. B. Maclaren.

would probably be a mistake to speak as if it were at once to him all that it afterwards became, yet, since he was of all men the most clubbable, from the beginning it gave him ample opportunities of acquaintance with men of various tastes, many of them of great ability, even if they had not yet achieved or were not achieving a reputation. Some of the members he already knew. Sir Charles Dilke and Mr. Andrew Lang he had previously met in the Riviera; Professor Masson was an Edinburgh friend of the family; to Dr. Appleton, editor of the *Academy*, and Mr. Walter Pollock, editor of the *Saturday Review*, he was soon introduced; but it would be long to enumerate the friends, and idle to recapitulate the acquaintances, that Stevenson soon made within those walls.

Into formal society nothing would ever have induced him to go in London any more than in Edinburgh; he invariably refused the opportunities which presented themselves to him, as they sooner or later have always presented themselves to young men with any reputation for social gifts and original conversation. In 1874, when he came to London for the first time under new auspices, he seems to have met a few well-known people; to have been taken to see Burne-Jones's pictures, then strictly withheld from any chance of public recognition; to have met Miss Thackeray, Mrs. Lynn Linton, and a few other ladies, chiefly at the house of Mr. Leslie Stephen, to whom he had been introduced by Mr. Colvin. His great and natural desire to see Carlyle was frustrated, for Mr. Stephen, on whose kind offices he depended, found the sage in one of his darker moods and at a moment of irritation. He had just been suffering at the hands of an interviewer for whom he fancied Mr. Stephen was responsible, and when Stevenson was mentioned as a young Scot who was most anxious to meet him, and who had taken to the study of Knox, the senior would only say that he did not see why anybody should want either to see his "wretched old carcase" or to say anything more about Knox, and that the young man had better apply when he had put his studies into an articulate shape.

Besides the visits to London and Cambridge there were many journeys and excursions;[1] and the importance of such travel to him in these days may be estimated by the degree in which it formed the topic of his early writings. Between 1871 and 1876 no less than nine of his papers deal with travel or the external appearance of places known to him; and it is scarcely necessary to remind the reader that his first three books were the *Inland Voyage*, the *Picturesque Notes on Edinburgh*, and the *Travels with a Donkey in the Cévennes*.

In the autumn of 1874 he joined his parents in an expedition to Chester and Barmouth, and in October took the walk in Buckinghamshire described the following spring in the *Portfolio* under the title of "An Autumn Effect." This ended, as a matter of fact, with his only visit to Oxford;[2] but Oxford and Cambridge left no more trace in his work than, at an earlier age,

---

[1] A pencil list of towns in which he had slept, compiled about 1886, to relieve the tedium of illness, gives the following totals: — England, 46 towns — 19 more than once; Scotland, 50 — 23 more than once; France, 74 — 31 more than once; the rest of Europe, 40 — 16 more than once.

[2] Unless it were another time when he visited Mr. Lang at Merton. The visit to Oxford is not mentioned in the *Portfolio*, but in a letter to his mother.

Rome or Naples or Venice. A reference to the chimes of the one, a conversation (in an unpublished novel) carried on at the other, and a few general remarks about the contrast between Scotch and English universities are all that is to be found about them in his writings.

In 1875 came the walk up the valley of the Loing with Sir Walter Simpson, in which Stevenson's costume led to the incarceration described in the *Epilogue to An Inland Voyage*, and this trip being cut short, he joined his parents, as he had intended, at Wiesbaden, and went with them to Homburg and Mainz.

In 1876 he spent the second week in January walking in Carrick and Galloway, when he slept a night at Ballantrae, and later in the year, after a visit in August to the Jenkins near Loch Carron, he joined Sir Walter Simpson again and took the canoe journey of the *Inland Voyage* from Antwerp to Brussels, and then from the French frontier by the Oise almost to the Seine.

These journeys and the general change in Stevenson's life were rendered possible, as I have said, by the liberality of his father (some ten years later he wrote, " I fall always on my feet; but I am constrained to add that the best part of my legs seems to be my father"[2]), yet it must not be supposed that Stevenson even now was often in funds. He was open-handed to a fault; and he had many wants of his own which often went unsatisfied. It is to this period that a story belongs which he was fond of telling against himself. He was staying in London, and had protracted his visit to the

[1] *Juvenilia*, p. 169.   [2] May, 1885.

extreme limit of his resources. On his way back to the North he arrived at the station with a sum barely sufficient for the cheapest ticket, available only by a night journey, and a newly bought copy of Mr. Swinburne's *Queen Mother and Rosamond.* On learning his deficiency, he tried his best powers of persuasion on the booking-clerk, but in vain: the man, in his blindness, refused to accept the book as any part of the payment, and, if I remember right, Stevenson passed the day in the station without food, and reached home next morning in a famished condition.

Thus, as we have seen, with the exception of his release from law and the friendship with Mr. Henley, conditions in Edinburgh remained much the same; the Savile and the people he met there were, together with Mr. Colvin's advice and help, the principal feature of his life in England; it is to France that we must turn for the other influences chiefly affecting him, and for the circumstances of most importance in determining his development at this period. In the winter of 1873–74 he had, as we have seen, renewed acquaintance with the Riviera, which in later days was to become yet more familiar. For the present he returned to that neighbourhood no more, but there was no year from 1874 to 1879 in which he did not pay one or more visits of several weeks' duration to another part of France. Except for the time that he was in the Cévennes and on his cruise down the Oise, he stayed mostly in the outskirts of the forest of Fontainebleau, in the valley of the Loing, or in Paris itself. Sometimes, as at Monastier, he was alone; sometimes, as at Nemours or at Cernay la Ville, he was with his cousin Bob or Sir Walter Simpson; but for the most part he lived in familiar intercourse with the artists who frequented his favourite resorts. The life was congenial to him, and his companions understood his temperament, if they did not necessarily appreciate his passion for letters. French was the only foreign tongue he ever mastered, and in that he acquired real proficiency. His knowledge of the language and literature was considerable, and its influence on his work was entirely for good, as it increased the delicacy and clearness of his style, and yet left his originality unimpaired.

It was the country again which seems to have affected him most and not the city; in both he lived with the same intimates, but though Paris might be the more exciting, yet at Fontainebleau he came with lasting results under the influence of the forest, and from it he carried away many vital memories.[1]

When his friends were painting, he often betook himself to lonely walks and meditations among the heaths and woods, but company and conversation counted for a great deal. "I knew three young men who walked together daily for some two months in a solemn and beautiful forest and in cloudless summer weather; daily they talked with unabated zest, and yet scarce wandered that whole time beyond two subjects—theology and love."[2]

His earliest and perhaps his most frequent haunt was Barbizon. It had been the home of Millet, and its fields were the scene of the *Angelus*. In the village there existed an inn which was reserved for the artists,

[1] " Forest Notes," *Juvenilia*, p. 211.
[2] *Talk and Talkers*, p. 185.

a strange society compounded of all nationalities, in which French, English, and Americans predominated. Stevenson himself has described it in an essay.[1]

"I was for some time a consistent Barbizonian; *et ego in Arcadia vixi;* it was a pleasant season; and that noiseless hamlet lying close among the borders of the wood is for me, as for so many others, a green spot in memory. The great Millet was just dead; the green shutters of his modest house were closed; his daughters were in mourning. The date of my first verse was thus an epoch in the history of art.

"Siron's inn, that excellent artists' barrack, was managed upon easy principles. At any hour of the night, when you returned from wandering in the forest, you went to the billiard-room and helped yourself to liquors, or descended to the cellar and returned laden with beer or wine. The Sirons were all locked in slumber; there was none to check your inroads; only at the week's end a computation was made, the gross sum was divided, and a varying share set down to every lodger's name under the rubric, *estrats.* Upon the more long-suffering the larger tax was levied; and your bill lengthened in a direct proportion to the easiness of your disposition. At any hour of the morning, again, you could get your coffee or cold milk and set forth into the forest. The doves had perhaps wakened you, fluttering into your chamber; and on the threshold of the inn you were met by the aroma of the forest. Close by were the great aisles, the mossy boulders, the interminable field of forest shadow. There you were free to dream and wander. And at

[1] "Fontainebleau," *Later Essays*, p. 212.

noon, and again at six o'clock, a good meal awaited you on Siron's table. The whole of your accommodation, set aside that varying item of the *estrats*, cost you five francs a day; your bill was never offered you until you asked for it; and if you were out of luck's way, you might depart for where you pleased and leave it pending.

"Theoretically, the house was open to all comers; practically, it was a kind of club. The guests protected themselves, and, in so doing, they protected Siron. Formal manners being laid aside, essential courtesy was the more rigidly exacted; the new arrival had to feel the pulse of the society; and a breach of its undefined observances was promptly punished. A man might be as plain, as dull, as slovenly, as free of speech as he desired; but to a touch of presumption or a word of hectoring these free Barbizonians were as sensitive as a tea-party of maiden ladies. I have seen people driven forth from Barbizon; it would be difficult to say in words what they had done, but they deserved their fate. They had shown themselves unworthy to enjoy these corporate freedoms; they had pushed themselves; they had 'made their head'; they wanted tact to appreciate the 'fine shades' of Barbizonian etiquette. And, once they were condemned, the process of extrusion was ruthless in its cruelty: after one evening with the formidable Bodmer, the Bailly of our commonwealth, the erring stranger was beheld no more; he rose exceeding early the next day, and the first coach conveyed him from the scene of his discomfiture. These sentences of banishment were never, in my knowledge, delivered against an artist; such would, I believe, have been illegal; but the odd and pleasant fact is this, that they were never needed. Painters, sculptors, writers, singers, I have seen all of these in Barbizon, and some were sulky, and some were blatant and inane; but one and all entered into the spirit of the association. . . .

"Our society, thus purged and guarded, was full of high spirits, of laughter, and of the initiative of youth. The few elder men who joined us were still young at heart, and took the key from their companions. We returned from long stations in the fortifying air, our blood renewed by the sunshine, our spirits refreshed by the silence of the forest; the Babel of loud voices sounded good; we fell to eat and play like the natural man; and in the high inn chamber, panelled with indifferent pictures, and lit by candles guttering in the night air, the talk and laughter sounded far into the night. It was a good place and a good life for any naturally minded youth; better yet for the student of painting, and perhaps best of all for the student of letters. He, too, was saturated in this atmosphere of style; he was shut out from the disturbing currents of the world; he might forget that there existed other and more pressing interests than that of art. But, in such a place, it was hardly possible to write; he could not drug his conscience, like the painter, by the production of listless studies; he saw himself idle among many who were apparently, and some who were really, employed; and what with the impulse of increasing health and the continual provocation of romantic scenes, he became tormented with the desire to work. He enjoyed a strenuous idleness full of visions, hearty meals, long, sweltering walks, mirth among companions; and, still floating like music through his brain, foresights of great works that Shakespeare might be proud to have conceived, headless epics, glorious torsos of dramas, and words that were alive with import. . . . We were all artists; almost all in the age of illusion, cultivating an imaginary genius, and walking to the strains of some deceiving Ariel; small wonder, indeed, if we were happy!"

Barbizon, however, was by no means the only resort of painters in this neighbourhood, nor the only one which Stevenson frequented: in the same paper he enumerates its rivals from his full knowledge. Marlotte, Montigny,[1] and Chailly-en-Bière he knew; Cernay la Ville was a favourite of his cousin Bob; but it was Grez which, in spite of an unpromising introduction, was his favourite quarters, and has the most important place in his history.

"Barbizon, Summer '75.

"MY DEAR MOTHER,—I have been three days at a place called Grez, a pretty and very melancholy village on the plain. A low bridge, with many arches choked with sedge; green fields of white and yellow waterlilies; poplars and willows innumerable; and about it all such an atmosphere of sadness and slackness, one could do nothing but get into the boat and out of it again, and yawn for bedtime. . . . I was very glad to be back again in this dear place, and smell the wet forest in the morning."

[1] Where Mr. W. H. Low's quarters summed up the delights of the Envoy to *Underwoods.*

157

But later he wrote how delightful it was "to awake in Grez, to go down the green inn-garden, to find the river streaming through the bridge, and to see the dawn begin across the poplared level. The meals are laid in the cool arbour, under fluttering leaves. The splash of oars and bathers, the bathing costumes out to dry, the trim canoes beside the jetty, tell of a society that has an eye to pleasure. There is 'something to do' at Grez. Perhaps, for that very reason, I can recall no such enduring ardours, no such glories of exhilaration, as among the solemn groves and uneventful hours of Barbizon. This 'something to do' is a great enemy to joy; it is a way out of it; you wreck your high spirits on some cut-and-dry employment, and behold them gone! But Grez is a merry place after its kind: pretty to see, merry to inhabit. The course of its pellucid river, whether up or down, is full of attractions for the navigator; the mirrored and inverted images of trees; lilies, and mills, and the foam and thunder of weirs. And of all noble sweeps of roadway, none is nobler, on a windy dusk, than the highroad to Nemours between its lines of talking poplar." [1]

Nemours itself he knew well, and there he often stayed. His first visit is described in a letter to his mother in 1875:—

"Nemours is a beautiful little town, watered by a great canal and a little river. The river is crossed by an infinity of little bridges, and the houses have courts and gardens, and come down in stairs to the very brim; and washerwomen sit everywhere in curious

[1] " Fontainebleau," *Later Essays*, p. 220; cf. *Juvenilia*, p. 199.

little penthouses and sheds. A sort of reminiscence
of Amsterdam. The old castle turned now into a ballroom and cheap theatre; the seats of the pit (the
places are 1f. and 2fs. in this theatre) are covered with
old Gobelins tapestry; one can still see heads in hel-
mets. In the actors' dressing-room are curious old
Henry Fourth looking-glasses. On the other hand, the
old manacles are now kept laid by in a box, with a lot
of flower-pots on the top of it, in a room with four
canary birds."

If the country had the more influence in the end,
Paris provided more variety and more diversion. There
Stevenson stayed, in all manner of lodgings, varying
from Meurice's Hotel (which was little to his liking) to
students' accommodation in the Quartier Latin, and
scattered throughout a region extending from Mont-
martre on the north to Mont Parnasse on the south.

At one time he writes: "I am in a new quarter, and
flâne about in a leisurely way. I dine every day in a
crèmerie with a party of Americans, an Irishman, and
sometimes an English lady." Again: "I am living
along with some fellows, and we partly make our own
food, and have great fun marketing." Another time:
"I have been engaged in a wild hunt for books — all
forenoon, all afternoon, with occasional returns to Rue
Racine with an armful. I have spent nearly all my
money; and if I have luck in to-day's hunt, I believe
I shall lay my head on the pillow to-night a beggar.
But I have had goodish luck, and a heap of nice books.
Please advance me £10 of my allowance. . . . Heaps
of articles growing before me. Hurray." An attempt
to work in some of the public libraries of Paris failed:

the face of officialism was too daunting. "They are worse than banks — if that be possible. . . . In public offices of all kinds I feel like Esther before Ahasuerus. I suspect there was some truth in my father's turkey-ing;[1] for the vice has descended to me."

This was the period when his letters were least frequent and least satisfactory, but of his sojourns in Paris no other memorial survives except the first chapters of *The Wrecker*, which partly in detail and wholly in spirit are drawn from Stevenson's recollections of these years. In addition I have collected a few fragments of letters and papers, which may help to eke out the scanty material for a picture of that time.

The first is a letter to his mother, describing a student's entertainment in the studio which was afterwards depicted in *Trilby*.

"MY DEAR MOTHER, — I was out last night at a party in a fellow's studio over in the Rue Notre Dame des Champs. Some of the people were in costume. One girl was so pretty and looked so happy that it did your heart good to see her. The studio looked very strange, lit with Chinese lanterns and a couple of strange lamps. The floor had been rubbed with candles, and was very slippery. O'Meara, in his character of young Donny-brook, tumbled about like a pair of old boots, and ——, for all he is so little, managed to fall into the arms of every girl he danced with, as he went round in the last figure of the quadrille. There was nothing to eat but sweet biscuits, and nothing to drink but syrup and water. It was a rum event."

The next was a typical holiday.

1 P. 21.

" *11th October, Paris.*— Here I am so far on my way
home. . . . Yesterday I had a splendid day. Luxem-
bourg in the morning. Breakfast. Bob, St. Gaudens the
sculptor, Low and I: hours of very good talk in the
French idiom. All afternoon in the Louvre, till they
turned us out unwilling. At night, the Français, *Rome
Vaincue,* an impossible play, with Sarah Bernhardt as
the blind grandmother, most sublime to behold. At
breakfast we had lobster mayonnaise, kidneys, brochet,
and tomates farcies, with lots of Carton. Dinner was a
mere hurried sustentation of the immortal spirit before
exposing it to another excitement. A splendid day,
but two running would not do."

The theatre was a source of great delight to him.
Although he had read (and written) plays from his early
years, had revelled in the melodramas of the toy-theatre,
and had acted with the Jenkins and in other private
theatricals, I find no reference to his having visited a
theatre before December, 1874, when he found Irving's
Hamlet "interesting (for it is really studied) but not
good"; and there is no sign of his having been really
impressed until he saw Salvini as Macbeth at Edinburgh
in the spring of 1876. Of this performance he wrote a
criticism for the *Academy,* which he afterwards condemned as dealing with a subject that was still beyond
the resources of his art.[1] He himself, I am told, was
never a tolerable actor, and certainly was never allotted
a part of any importance. But his enthusiasm for the
drama was great, and during these years was heightened
and instructed by the two chief friends who shared his
taste — Professor Jenkin and Mr. Henley.

He used to speak with delight of Delaunay's per-

[1] *Memoir of Fleeming Jenkin,* p. 145.

formance in a play by Alexandre Dumas, *Mademoiselle de Belleisle*, declaring that in calling out through a window on the stage to some one supposed to be in the castle-court below, Delaunay had succeeded in so modulating his voice as "to make you feel the cold night air and the moonlight."

One of his visits to the theatre led to a very characteristic scene, described long afterwards in a letter to Mr. Archer. The play had been the *Demi-Monde* of Dumas fils, in the last act of which Olivier de Jalin employs an unworthy stratagem against the woman who had been his mistress.

"I came forth from that performance in a breathing heat of indignation. . . . On my way down the Français stairs, I trod on an old gentleman's toes, whereupon, with that suavity which so well becomes me, I turned about to apologise, and on the instant, repenting me of that intention, stopped the apology midway, and added something in French to this effect: 'No, you are one of the *lâches* who have been applauding that piece. I retract my apology.' Said the old Frenchman, laying his hand on my arm, and with a smile that was truly heavenly in temperance, irony, good-nature, and knowledge of the world, 'Ah, monsieur, vous êtes bien jeune.'"[1]

To this time also belongs the story reported by Mr. Andrew Lang.[2] Stevenson, one day at a café, hearing a Frenchman say that the English were cowards, promptly hit him across the face. "Monsieur, vous m'avez frappé!" said the Gaul. "A ce qu'il paraît," said the Scot, and there the incident ended. It is an

[1] *Letters*, ii. 94. [2] *North American Review*, February, 1895.

instance the more of his fearlessness ; for although he would never have hesitated, he was quite incompetent to fight a duel with either pistol or sword.

The effect produced upon outsiders must sometimes have been rather bewildering. He used to tell how one day he and his cousin Bob, happening to be rather more in funds than usual, went to dine in one of the cafés of the Palais Royal. " The café was not very full," so I remember the story, "and there was nobody near us, but presently a gentleman and his wife came in and sat down at the next table. They were evidently people of good position, well dressed and distinguished in appearance. But they were talking French, and we paid not the slightest attention to them. We had lately got hold of the works of Thomas Aquinas, and our conversation was on the most extraordinary medley of subjects — on men, women, and things, with a very large leaven of mediæval theology, and on all we spoke in English with the most startling frankness and with the most bewildering transitions. Bob is the best talker in the world; I never knew him more brilliant, and I did my best.

" Those people sat and had their dinner and took not the slightest notice of us, but talked quietly to one another in Parisian French. Just before they got up to go, the gentleman turned to his wife and said to her in English without a trace of accent, 'My dear, won't you take anything more ? ' I have often wondered who they were, and what on earth they thought of us."

His deficiencies in letter-writing and his protracted absences from home led very naturally to protests from

his parents and especially from his mother.   The answer
was characteristic.

" Euston Hotel, 16th Oct., 1874.

"You must not be vexed at my absences.   You
must understand that I shall be a nomad, more or less,
until my days be done.   You don't know how much
I used to long for it in old days; how I used to go
and look at the trains leaving, and wish to go with
them.   And now, you know, that I have a little more
that is solid under my feet, you must take my nomadic
habits as a part of me.   Just wait till I am in swing,
and you will see that I shall pass more of my life with
you than elsewhere; only take me as I am, and give
me time.   I *must* be a bit of a vagabond; it's your own
fault, after all, is n't it?   You should n't have had a
tramp for a son."

While the man was in the making during these years,
the writer also was passing through the stages of a development which was unusually protracted.   The per-
fecting of his style was necessarily a work of time, but
in the meanwhile, if he had seen his way to use the
gifts at his command, his love of romance, his imagination, and his vivid interest in life might well have
enabled him to produce work which would have secured him immediate popularity and reward.

Nothing of the sort, however, was accomplished, and,
high as his standard always was, this delay may well
have been a gain for his ultimate success.   During the
six years between his first appearance as a printed and
paid author and the publication of the *Travels with a
Donkey*, his published work consisted of some six-and-

twenty magazine articles, chiefly critical and social essays, just half of which were in the *Cornhill Magazine;*
two small books of travel; two books in serial instalments, afterwards reprinted; and five short stories also
in periodicals. There were besides a few rejected articles, a certain amount of journalism, and at least
eight stories or novels, none of which ever saw the
light, as well as a play or two and some verses, a small
part of which were ultimately included in his published
works.

By this time Stevenson had left behind him the early
stages of apprenticeship, and far as he still was from
satisfying his own taste and aims, there is no longer
any possibility of pointing out the definite stages
through which he passed year by year, or the methods
of work which he employed.

A list of his writings will be found in the Appendix,
arranged under separate years. It is therefore unnecessary in this place to do more than record his general
progress, adding merely a detached note on any point
of interest as it arises, or quoting his own criticisms,
which, for the most part, are singularly shrewd and
free from bias.

In September, 1873, he wrote: "There is no word
of 'Roads'; I suspect the *Saturday Review* must have
looked darkly upon it — so be it; we must just try to
do something better." And so, as we have seen, the
article appeared in the *Portfolio* for December. Three
weeks later, in a letter to his mother, he expressed the
opinion that "it is quite the best thing I have ever
done, to my taste. There are things expressed in it far
harder to express than in anything else I ever had; and

that, after all, is the great point.   As for style, *ça vien-dra peut-être.*"

In 1874 he had five articles in four different maga-zines: these included "Ordered South" in *Macmillan's*, and, still more important, the paper on "Victor Hugo's Romances" in the *Cornhill*.   The former, which took him three months to write, was his first work ever re-published in its original form; the latter, which was anonymous, but afterwards reappeared in *Familiar Studies of Men and Books*, marked, in his own judg-ment, the beginning of his command of style.   Long afterwards in Samoa, in answer to a question, he told me that in this essay he had first found himself able to say several things in the way in which he felt they should be said.   It may also be noticed that this was his first appearance in the magazine which by the dis-cernment of Mr. Leslie Stephen did so much for him in taking his early work.

This year he proposed to himself, and began to read for, a book on four great Scotsmen — Knox, Hume, Burns, and Scott.   All that ever came of it, and he had the subjects a long time in his mind, were the essays on Burns and Knox, which dealt only with one aspect of either character.   At this time he was working at an essay on Walt Whitman, but his views did not find expression till 1878.   The papers on Knox were read before the Speculative Society in November, 1874, and January, 1875.   Late in the former year he was mak-ing another assault upon the stronghold of the Novel with a tale called "When the Devil was Well," deal-ing with the adventures of an Italian sculptor of the fif-teenth century.   It was finished the next year, and the unfavourable opinion of his friends was accepted as final.

1875 saw nothing published except two double articles, the "Autumn Effect" and "Knox," the notice of Béranger in the *Encyclopædia Britannica*, and the pamphlet entitled *An Appeal to the Clergy of the Church of Scotland*. This last had been set up in type the preceding autumn, and was an appeal to the Scottish clergy to use the Church Patronage Act of 1874 as an opportunity for effacing differences between their own communion and the dissenting bodies, and to do all in their power to restore religious unity.

In January, 1875, Stevenson proposed to the *Academy* a series of papers on the Parnassiens — de Banville, Coppée, Soulary, and Prudhomme — and when this was not accepted, he devoted a good deal of his time to the study of the French literature of the fifteenth century, which resulted in the articles on Villon and Charles of Orleans. He was filled with enthusiasm for Joan of Arc, a devotion and also a cool-headed admiration which he never lost. He projected a series of articles which should include the Maid, Louis XI., and René of Anjou. The same reading led to the experiments in the French verse metres of that date which were almost contemporary with the work of Mr. Andrew Lang and Mr. Austin Dobson, who brought the Ballade and Rondeau back to favour in England. Stevenson, however, never published any of these attempts, and except two translations published in the *Letters*, and one set preserved by Mr. Lang, I believe the characteristic verses at the head of this chapter are the only finished piece which survives.

A prose poem on "The Spirit of the Spring" unfortunately went astray, but one or two short studies of the same date and in a similar vein indicate that it was no masterpiece. After the Italian story was finished, he took up one of his old tales called *A Country Dance*, which likewise came to nothing; and also wrote *The Story of King Matthias' Hunting Horn*, of which I only know that it was "wild and fantastic."

As the result of a condensation of Burns's life and a criticism of his works for the *Encyclopædia Britannica*, the famous Scotsmen had now become "Ramsay, Fergusson, and Burns." The editor of the *Encyclopædia* found the Burns too critical, and too much at variance with the accepted Scottish tradition, and though payment was made for it, it was not used. Stevenson wrote: "*8th June, 1876.*—I suppose you are perfectly right in saying there was a want of enthusiasm about the article. To say truth, I had, I fancy, an exaggerated idea of the gravity of an encyclopædia, and wished to give mere bones, and to make no statements that should seem even warm. And perhaps, also, I may have a little latent cynicism, which comes out when I am at work. I believe you are right in saying I had not said enough of what is highest and best in him. Such a topic is disheartening; the clay feet are easier dealt with than the golden head."

To 1876 we owe the only piece of dramatic criticism that Stevenson ever published, and four articles in the *Cornhill Magazine*, which from this time onward marked all his contributions to its pages with the initials R. L. S. The full names of a few very eminent authors had been given from the commencement; but about the beginning of Mr. Leslie Stephen's editorship, in 1871, a second rank of distinction was established by allowing an equally small number of writers to denote their articles by their initials. All Stevenson's papers except the first (1874) were thus distinguished; and though the R. L. S. caused them at first to be frequently attributed to the editor, yet it was under these initials that Stevenson first won recognition in the select circle which knew and appreciated literature.

A novel, *The Hair Trunk, or The Ideal Commonwealth*, was begun and partly carried out at this time. A party of friends meeting at Cambridge proposes to form a colony, which is to be established in "Navigator's Island"—Samoa, of all places—of which the author had heard only the year before from his connection, the Hon. J. Seed, formerly Secretary to the Customs and Marine Departments of New Zealand,[1] who had been sent to report upon the islands by the New Zealand Government. *In the Windbound Arethusa* was another attempt of the same date which attained no better result.

The year 1876 thrice saw the rejection of the article on "Some Portraits by Raeburn," afterwards included in *Virginibus Puerisque*. It was refused in turn by the *Cornhill*, the *Pall Mall Gazette*, and *Blackwood's Magazine*, though it is only fair to Mr. Stephen to say that he helped the author in trying to place it elsewhere. It was seldom that Stevenson either continued, or was driven, to try his fortune elsewhere with a rejected article. But this case is all the more interesting because he tried again and again, and was clearly in

[1] *Letters*, i. 95.

the right. Editors cannot always follow their judgment or their inclinations, but articles such as the
Raeburn seldom come their way.

The event of the year was, of course, the canoe
voyage. Stevenson, as we have already seen, had for
some time shared his friends' taste for navigating the
Firth of Forth in these craft, which the enthusiasm of
"Rob Roy" Macgregor had made popular ten years
before. A good deal of time was spent, as we have
seen, on the river at Grez, and canoes were introduced
there by the English colony, headed by Sir Walter
Simpson and his brother, and by R. A. M. Stevenson,
who devised a leather canoe of his own "with a niche
for everything," and, as his friends said, "a place for
nothing." Mr. Warington Baden-Powell had published
in the pages of the *Cornhill Magazine* in 1870 the log
of the *Nautilus* and *Isis* canoes on a journey through
Sweden and on the Baltic. But the idea of the journey
itself seems to have been suggested by *Our Autumn
Holiday on French Rivers*, by Mr. J. L. Molloy, published in 1874, the account of a journey up the Seine
and down the Loire in a four-oared outrigger.

That the cruise itself was on the whole rather a cheer-
less experience, is seen by the following letter, in which
Stevenson lets us behind the scenes, and for once even
grumbles a little.

"*Compiègne, 9th Sept., 1876.* [*Canoe Voyage.*]
"We have had deplorable weather quite steady ever
since the start; not one day without heavy showers;
and generally much wind and cold wind forbye. . . .
I must say it has sometimes required a stout heart; and

sometimes one could not help sympathising inwardly with the French folk who hold up their hands in astonishment over our pleasure journey.   Indeed I do not know that I would have stuck to it as I have done, if it had not been for professional purposes; for an easy book may be written and sold, with mighty little brains about it, where the journey is of a certain seriousness and can be named.   I mean, a book about a journey from York to London must be clever; a book about the Caucasus may be what you will.   Now I mean to make this journey at least a curious one; it won't be finished these vacations.

"Hitherto a curious one it has been; and above all in its influence on S. and me.   I wake at six every morning; and we are generally in bed and asleep before half-past nine.   Last night I found my way to my room with a dark cloud of sleep over my shoulders, so thick that the candle burnt red at about the hour of 8.40.   If that is n't healthy, egad, I wonder what is."

CHAPTER VII

TRANSITION — 1876–79

" You may paddle all day long ; but it is when you come back at nightfall, and look in at the familiar room, that you find Love or Death awaiting you beside the stove ; and the most beautiful adventures are not those we go to seek."

The concluding words of " An Inland Voyage."

THE next three years of Stevenson's life were so closely similar to the three preceding, that at first sight, but for his own selection of the age of five-and-twenty as the limit of youth, it might seem almost unnecessary to make any division between them. He continued to spend his time between France, London, and Edinburgh, to lead a more or less independent life, and to give the best of his talents and industry to his now recognised profession. The year 1877 was marked by the acceptance of the first of his stories ever printed — *A Lodging for the Night* — and from that date his fiction began to take its place beside, and gradually to supersede, the essays with which his career had opened. The month of May, 1878, saw not only the appearance of his first book — *An Inland Voyage* — but also the beginning of his two first serial publications — the *New Arabian Nights* and the *Picturesque Notes on Edinburgh;* and they were followed at the end of the year by the *Edinburgh* in book form, and in June, 1879, by the *Travels with a Donkey.* All these, however, were but a measure of the author's growing reputation, and of the facility with which he could now find a publisher.

Original as these writings were, and unlike the work of his contemporaries, none of them constituted any new departure in his life or any alteration in his attitude to the world: and the change that now came arrived from another quarter. His friendships, as we have seen, counted for a great deal with Stevenson, and though the roll of them was not yet closed, and ended indeed only at his death, it was at the beginning of this period that he made the acquaintance which affected him more than any other—he now met for the first time the lady who was afterwards to be his wife.

Already it is becoming difficult to realise that there was a time not long distant when study for all the professions, including that of art, was hedged about with arbitrary restrictions for women. At the date of which I am speaking these limitations had been removed to some extent in Paris as far as the studios were concerned, but the natural consequences had not yet followed in country quarters, and women artists were as yet unknown in any of the colonies about Fontainebleau. Hitherto these societies had been nearly as free from the female element as were afterwards the early novels of Stevenson himself: the landlady, the chambermaid, the peasant girl passed across the stage, but the leading rôles were filled by men alone. But when Stevenson and Sir Walter Simpson, the "Arethusa" and the "Cigarette," returned from the Inland Voyage to their quarters at Grez, they found the colony in trepidation at the expected arrival of the invader.

The new-comers, however, were neither numerous nor formidable; being only an American lady and her two children—a young girl and a boy. Mrs. Osbourne had seen her domestic happiness break up in California, and had come to France for the education of her family. She and her daughter had thrown themselves with ardour into the pursuit of painting, and thus became acquainted with some of the English and American artists in Paris. After profiting by the opportunities afforded them in the capital, they were in search of country lodgings, and accordingly, having taken counsel with their artist friends, they came to Grez.

So here for the first time Stevenson saw the woman whom Fate had brought half-way across the world to meet him. He straightway fell in love; he knew his own mind, and in spite of all dissuasions and difficulties, his choice never wavered. The difficulties were so great and hope so remote that nothing was said to his parents or to any but two or three of his closest friends. But in the meantime life took on a cheerful hue, and the autumn passed brightly for them all until the middle of October,[1] when Stevenson must return to Edinburgh, there to spend the winter.

In January, 1877, he came to London for a fortnight, and first met Mr. Gosse, who, being immediately added to the ranks of his intimate friends, has given us a most vivid and charming description of the effect produced on strangers at that time by Stevenson.

"It was in 1877,[2] or late in 1876, that I was presented to Stevenson, at the old Savile Club, by Mr. Sidney Colvin, who thereupon left us to our devices. We

---

[1] To the next year belongs the charcoal drawing made by Mrs. Osbourne of her future husband, which has been redrawn by Mr. T. Blake Wirgman, and stands at the beginning of this volume.

[2] *Critical Kitcats* (London, William Heinemann, 1896), p. 278.

went downstairs and lunched together, and then we adjourned to the smoking-room. As twilight came on I tore myself away, but Stevenson walked with me across Hyde Park, and nearly to my house. He had an engagement, and so had I, but I walked a mile or two back with him. The fountains of talk had been unsealed, and they drowned the conventions. I came home dazzled with my new friend, saying, as Constance does of Arthur, 'Was ever such a gracious creature born ?'

".... Those who have written about him from later impressions than those of which I speak, seem to me to give insufficient prominence to the gaiety of Stevenson. It was his cardinal quality in those early days. A childlike mirth leaped and danced in him; he seemed to skip upon the hills of life. He was simply bubbling with quips and jests; his inherent earnestness or passion about abstract things was incessantly relieved by jocosity; and when he had built one of his intellectual castles in the sand, a wave of humour was certain to sweep in and destroy it. I cannot, for the life of me, recall any of his jokes; and written down in cold blood, they might not be funny if I did. They were not wit so much as humanity, the many-sided outlook upon life. I am anxious that his laughter-loving mood should not be forgotten, because later on it was partly, but I think never wholly, quenched by ill-health, responsibility, and the advance of years. He was often, in the old days, excessively and delightfully silly—silly with the silliness of an inspired schoolboy; and I am afraid that our laughter sometimes sounded ill in the ears of age. . . .

175

" My experience of Stevenson during these first years was confined to London, upon which he would make sudden piratical descents, staying a few days or weeks, and melting into air again. He was much at my house; and it must be told that my wife and I, as young married people, had possessed ourselves of a house too large for our slender means immediately to furnish. The one person who thoroughly approved of our great, bare, absurd drawing-room was Louis, who very earnestly dealt with us on the immorality of chairs and tables, and desired us to sit always, as he delighted to sit, upon hassocks on the floor. Nevertheless, as armchairs and settees straggled into existence, he handsomely consented to use them, although never in the usual way, but with his legs thrown sideways over the arms of them, or the head of a sofa treated as a perch. In particular, a certain shelf, with cupboards below, attached to a bookcase, is worn with the person of Stevenson, who would spend half an evening while passionately discussing some great question of morality or literature, leaping sideways in a seated posture to the length of this shelf, and then back again. He was eminently peripatetic, too, and never better company than walking in the street, this exercise seeming to inflame his fancy."

It was in these years especially that he gave the impression of something transitory and unreal, sometimes almost inhuman.

" He was careful, as I have hardly known any other man to be, not to allow himself to be burdened by the weight of material things. It was quite a jest with us that he never acquired any possessions. In the midst of those who produced books, pictures, prints, *bric-à-brac*, none of these things ever stuck to Stevenson. There are some deep-sea creatures, the early part of whose life is spent dancing through the waters; at length some sucker or tentacle touches a rock, adheres, pulls down more tentacles, until the creature is caught there, stationary for the remainder of its existence. So it happens to men, and Stevenson's friends caught the ground with a house, a fixed employment, a 'stake in life'; he alone kept dancing in the free element, unattached."[1]

These were the days when he most frequented the Savile Club, and the lightest and most vivacious part of him there came to the surface. He might spend the morning in work or business, and would then come to the club for luncheon. If he were so fortunate as to find any congenial companions disengaged, or to induce them to throw over their engagements, he would lead them off to the smoking-room, and there spend an afternoon in the highest spirits and the most brilliant and audacious talk.

His private thoughts and prospects must often have been of the gloomiest, but he seems to have borne his unhappiness with a courage as high as he ever afterwards displayed, and with a show of levity which imposed on his friends and often ended by carrying him out of himself.

The whim of independence to which Mr. Gosse refers was carried out to an extreme by the two Stevenson cousins, about this time, in one of their visits to Paris, an experience which Louis afterwards transferred to the pages of *The Wrecker*. " Stennis," it may be

[1] *Critical Kitcats* (London, William Heinemann, 1896), p. 300.

LIFE OF ROBERT LOUIS STEVENSON

explained, was the nearest approach to their name possible to Barbizon, and accordingly it was as Stennis *aîné*
and Stennis *frère* that the pair were always known.

"The two Stennises had come from London, it appeared, a week before with nothing but greatcoats and
tooth-brushes. It was expensive, to be sure, for every
time you had to comb your hair a barber must be paid,
and every time you changed your linen one shirt must
be bought and another thrown away; but anything
was better, argued these young gentlemen, than to be
the slaves of haversacks. 'A fellow has to get rid
gradually of all material attachments: that was manhood,' said they; 'and as long as you were bound
down to anything—house, umbrella, or portmanteau—
you were still tethered by the umbilical cord.'" [1]

When he broke through this rule, his inconsistency
was equally original and unexpected.

"*Paris, Jan., 1878.*—I have become a bird fancier.
I carry six little creatures no bigger than my thumb
about with me almost all the day long; they are so pretty;
and it is so nice to waken in the morning and hear them
sing." Six or seven years later he again alludes to these
or to other similar pets. "There is only one sort of
bird that I can tolerate caged, though even then I think
it hard, and that is what is called in France the Bec-
d'Argent. I once had two of these pigmies in captivity;
and in the quiet, bare house upon a silent street where
I was then living, their song, which was not much
louder than a bee's, but airily musical, kept me in a
perpetual good-humour. I put the cage upon my table
when I worked, carried it with me when I went for

[1] *The Wrecker*, i. 73.

meals, and kept it by my head at night: the first thing in the morning, these *maestrini* would pipe up."

The following letter written from Paris has preserved a record of one of the thousand little kind and thoughtful acts which were so characteristic of Stevenson. Most of them are nameless and unremembered, but this — thanks to his perception of its humour — has been handed down to us.

"*1st Feb., 1877, Paris.*—MY DEAR MOTHER,—I have ordered a picture. There is magnificence for you. Poor —— is, as usual, hard up, and I knew wanted to make me a present of a sketch; so I took the first word and offered him 50f. for one. You should have seen us. I was so embarrassed that I could not finish a single phrase, and kept beginning, 'You know,' and 'You understand,' and 'Look here, ——,' and ending in pitiful intervals of silence. I was perspiring all over. Suddenly I saw —— begin to break out all over in a silvery dew; and he just made a dive at me and took me in his arms — in a kind of champion comique style, you know, but with genuine feeling."

This letter is also an indirect confirmation of what has been said in the preceding chapter as to Stevenson's poverty. About this time, however, his father followed the precedent set in his own case, and paid to Louis as an instalment of his patrimony a considerable sum, amounting, I believe, to not less than a thousand pounds. The fact is certain, the date and exact details have been lost. In the end Stevenson derived small benefit himself. "The little money he had," as Mr. Colvin says, "was always absolutely at the disposal of his friends." In 1877 he had still £800, but, owing to misfortunes befalling his friends, in none of which was he under any obligation to intervene, within less than two years nothing of it remained. His income from writing was as yet extremely small, the payment for his essays amounting to a guinea a page, so that until 1878 he probably from all sources had never made £50 in any one year.

As to his work, the actual output of 1877 was no more than one contribution to *Temple Bar* and three *Cornhill* articles, of which the *Apology for Idlers* had been rejected for *Macmillan's* the year before. The *Temple Bar* story — *A Lodging for the Night*, already mentioned — was the outcome of his studies for the essay on Villon in the *Cornhill* for August, and the last result of his attention to French mediæval literature. But of his acumen and insight into Villon's character (on which recent discoveries have thrown fresh light), the specialists can hardly find enough to say.[1]

If this year had little to show, it was only because much of it was spent in preparing for the next year's harvest. 1878 was at once in quantity and in quality the richest year he had yet known. *An Inland Voyage* was published in May: the journey with the donkey was taken, and an elaborate diary of it kept: there were four essays and a story in *Cornhill;* three essays, a story, and the *New Arabian Nights* in *London;* a story in *Temple Bar;* while *Picturesque Notes on Edinburgh* ran in the *Portfolio* from June till December, and then came out in book form.

[1] Letter of M. Marcel Schwob to Mr. Colvin, *Literature*, November 4th, 1899.

London was a weekly journal, founded by Robert Glasgow Brown, Stevenson's colleague on the *Edinburgh University Magazine*,[1] and after December, 1877, edited by Mr. Henley, who some time before had left Edinburgh.

It was in page and type not unlike the *World*, and to the omniscience necessary to an ordinary weekly paper it added a strong flavour of literature. Much of Mr. Henley's lighter verse appeared first in its columns, and among its less irregular contributors were Mr. Andrew Lang and the late Grant Allen and James Runciman. It was a staunch opponent of Mr. Gladstone and all his works, and won the favourable notice of Lord Beaconsfield. But the foundations of its finance were laid in sand, and it survived its originator little more than a year. It was the first paper edited by Mr. Henley, but though he never admitted to his columns work more brilliant of its kind, the *Arabian Nights* series was supposed by more than one of the proprietors sufficiently to account for the unpopularity of their journal.[2]

The conception of these stories is recorded in a letter to R. A. M. Stevenson. "The first idea of all was the hansom cabs, which I communicated to you in your mother's drawing-room in Chelsea. The same afternoon the Prince de Galles and the Suicide Club were invented, and several more now forgotten." The first half was actually written partly at Burford Bridge, partly at Swanston, while the *Rajah's Diamond* was

[1] *Memories and Portraits*, p. 128.
[2] L. Cope Cornford. *Robert Louis Stevenson*, p. 51. W. Blackwood & Sons, 1899.

written at Monastier, before the author set out with his *ânesse*. *The Sire de Malétroit's Door* (Door being substituted for the original "Mousetrap") was invented in France, first told over the fire one evening in Paris, and ultimately written at Penzance.

Providence and the Guitar was based upon a story told by a strolling French actor and his Bulgarian wife, who had stayed at Grez. The man had played inferior parts at a good theatre, and the woman also had been on the stage. They were quiet, innocent creatures, who spent all the daytime in fishing in the river. They had their meals on a bare table in the kitchen, and in the evening they sang in the dining-room and had a little "tombola" as in the story. They made the best of the most hideous poverty, but the worst of it was that they were forced to leave their only child with a peasant woman, while they were tramping from village to village. She had let the child fall, and it was in consequence a hunchback. Stevenson had much talk with them, taking great pleasure in their company and delight in hearing of their experiences. But there is no further foundation for the legend that he went strolling with them, or ever acted to a French audience.

When the story appeared he sent to the pair the money it brought him, and he received a most charming letter of thanks, which unfortunately has disappeared.

In 1877, Stevenson, having spent part of February and of June and July in France, returned there again from August to November. He did not carry out his original project of another canoe voyage by the Loing, the Loire, the Saone, and the Rhône to the Mediterranean, but spent some time with Sir Walter Simpson either at Nemours or at Moret where the Loing joins the Seine. Their experience of the Oise had suggested the charms of the life on board a barge, their imagination was kindled, nothing would content them but to acquire such a vessel for themselves, well found in all things they could desire, picturesque and romantic as craft had never yet been; and in this fashion they should make a leisurely progress along the waterways of Europe.

"There should be no white fresher, and no green more emerald than ours, in all the navy of the canals. There should be books in the cabin, and tobacco jars, and some old Burgundy as red as a November sunset, and as fragrant as a violet in April."

The *Eleven Thousand Virgins of Cologne* was "procured and christened," but on that cruise and under that flag she never started. A financial difficulty arose, and both barge and canoes alike had to be sold. So Stevenson's only other travelling this year was a trip with his parents to Cornwall, when he went as far as the Scilly Islands with his mother.

In 1878 he seems to have spent no more than a fortnight in Scotland until December, although he was in London four or five times. In April he stayed with his parents at the inn at Burford Bridge, under Box Hill, " with its arbours and green garden and silent, eddying river," " known already as the place where Keats wrote some of his *Endymion*, and Nelson parted from his Emma," and connected hereafter, it may be, with the *New Arabian Nights*, and the friendship between Stevenson and Mr. George Meredith, of which this

visit saw the beginning. All this summer he was acting as private secretary to Professor Fleeming Jenkin,
who was a juror at the International Exhibition at Paris;
the only post approaching any regular position or employment that Stevenson ever held.

This intimate association with his friend was a great
delight to them both, and in no respect more than in
the indulgence of their taste for the theatre.

"Another unalloyed dramatic pleasure, which Fleeming and I shared in the year of the Paris Exposition,
was the *Marquis de Villemer*, that blameless play, per-
formed by Madeleine Brohan, Delaunay, Worms, and
Broisat — an actress, in such parts at least, to whom I
have never seen full justice rendered. He had his fill
of weeping on that occasion; and when the piece was
at an end, in front of a café in the mild midnight air, we
had our fill of talk about the art of acting." [1]

Of an earlier experience in the same year, Stevenson
writes:—

"I have been to see Salvini, and I now know more
about him; no diminution of respect, rather an increase,
from being able to compare him with the Français
people, but a more critical vein. I notice, above all,
the insufficiency, the scholastic key of his gestures, as
compared with the incomparable freedom and inspiration of his intonations. As for Sarah Bernhardt, although her fame is only now beginning to reach England, and is now greater than ever in France, she is but
the ghost of herself; and those who have not seen her
before will never see her again — never see her at all, I
mean."

[1] *Memoir of Fleeming Jenkin*, p. 145.

Meanwhile he was working hard, in spite of a touch of illness for which the doctor nearly ordered him to leave Paris for the South of France. *An Inland Voyage* had been accepted by Messrs. Kegan Paul, Trench & Co. at the beginning of the year; and on the 17th February we find the author writing from Paris: "I have now been four days writing a — preface, a weary preface." But it was that which stands before the *Inland Voyage*, and his readers have little reason to regret the amount of time so employed.

A week later he says: "I am getting a lot of work ready in my mind, and as soon as I am able to square my elbows, I shall put it through my hands rapidly. What a blessing work is! I don't think I could face life without it; and how glad I am I took to literature! It helps me so much."

In the whirl of Paris, during the same month, he wrote this letter to his father, sitting at a café in the Quartier Latin:—

> "*Café de la Source, Bd. St. Michel, Paris,
> 15th Feb., 1878.*
>
> "A thought has come into my head which I think would interest you. Christianity is, among other things, a very wise, noble, and strange doctrine of life. Nothing so difficult to specify as the position it occupies with regard to asceticism. It is not ascetic. Christ was of all doctors (if you will let me use the word) one of the least ascetic. And yet there is a theory of living in the gospels which is curiously indefinable, and leans towards asceticism on one side, although it leans away from it on the other. In fact, asceticism is used

therein as a means, not as an end. The wisdom of this world consists in making oneself very little in order to avoid many knocks; in preferring others, in order that, even when we lose, we shall find some pleasure in the event; in putting our desires outside of ourselves, in another ship, so to speak, so that, when the worst happens, there will be something left. You see, I speak of it as a doctrine of life, and as a wisdom for this world. People must be themselves, I suppose. I feel every day as if religion had a greater interest for me; but that interest is still centred on the little rough-and-tumble world in which our fortunes are cast for the moment. I cannot transfer my interests, not even my religious interests, to any different sphere. . . . I have had some sharp lessons and some very acute sufferings in these last seven-and-twenty years — more even than you would guess. I begin to grow an old man; a little sharp, I fear, and a little close and unfriendly; but still I have a good heart, and believe in myself and my fellow-men and the God who made us all. . . . There are not many sadder people in the world, perhaps, than I. I have my eye on a sick-bed;[1] I have written letters to-day that it hurt me to write, and I fear it will hurt others to receive; I am lonely and sick and out of heart. Well, I still hope; I still believe; I still see the good in the inch, and cling to it. It is not much, perhaps, but it is always something.

"I find I have wandered a thousand miles from what I meant. It was this: of all passages bearing on Christianity in that form of a worldly wisdom, the most Christian, and, so to speak, the key of the whole posi-

[1] R. Glasgow Brown lay dying in the Riviera.

tion, is the Christian doctrine of revenge. And it appears that this came into the world through Paul! There is a fact for you. It was to speak of this that I began this letter; but I have got into deep seas and must go on.

" There is a fine text in the Bible, I don't know where, to the effect that all things work together for good to those who love the Lord. . . . Strange as it may seem to you, everything has been, in one way or the other, bringing me a little nearer to what I think you would like me to be. 'T is a strange world, indeed, but there is a manifest God for those who care to look for him.

" This is a very solemn letter for my surroundings in this busy café; but I had it on my heart to write it; and, indeed, I was out of the humour for anything lighter. — Ever your affectionate son,

" ROBERT LOUIS STEVENSON.

" *P. S.* — While I am writing gravely, let me say one word more. I have taken a step towards more intimate relations with you. But don't expect too much of me. . . . Try to take me as I am. This is a rare moment, and I have profited by it; but take it as a rare moment. Usually I hate to speak of what I really feel, to that extent that when I find myself *cornered,* I have a tendency to say the reverse.   R. L. S."

This graver tone was beginning to grow upon him, for all his spirits and light-heartedness. It seemed, indeed, as if happiness had shown him her face only that he might be filled with inextinguishable longing and regret. Mrs. Osbourne had hitherto remained in France, but this year she returned to California.   All was dark before them. She was not free to follow her inclination, and though the step of seeking a divorce was open to her, yet the interests and feelings of others had to be considered, and for the present all idea of a union was impossible. Stevenson, on his side, was still far from earning his own livelihood, and could not expect his parents to give their assistance or even their consent to the marriage. So there came the pain of parting without prospect of return, and he who was afterwards so long an exile from his friends now suffered separation from his dearest by the breadth of a continent and an ocean.

At first he continued to lead his life as if nothing had happened. After his Exhibition work was over, he went to Monastier, a mountain town near the sources of the Loire, and there occupied himself with a strenuous effort in completing both the *New Arabian Nights* and the *Picturesque Notes on Edinburgh*, both at this time in their serial career. There seems an irony in the fact that, having lived most of his life in Edinburgh, more or less against his will, he should retire to France only to write about it. But, as if by way of protest against realism, he never drew his native country or his countrymen better than when he was absent from Scotland.

At Monastier he spent some three weeks and completed his work, finding time also for some pencil sketches of the country and of the people, and obtaining, as always, a pleasant footing among the inhabitants, most of whom probably had never seen an Englishman (or Scotchman) in their lives.[1]

[1] *The Studio*, Winter Number, 1896–97; *Juvenilia*, p. 216.

On September 23rd he set out with his donkey on his eleven days' journey through the Cévennes, but here too his thoughts pursued him.

"I heard the voice of a woman singing some sad, old, endless ballad not far off. It seemed to be about love and a *bel amoureux*, her handsome sweetheart; and I wished I could have taken up the strain and answered her, as I went on upon my invisible woodland way, weaving, like Pippa in the poem, my own thoughts with hers. What could I have told her? Little enough; and yet all the heart requires. How the world gives and takes away, and brings sweethearts near only to separate them again into distant and strange lands; but to love is the great amulet which makes the world a garden; and 'hope, which comes to all,' outwears the accidents of life, and reaches with tremulous hand beyond the grave and death. Easy to say: yea, but also, by God's mercy, both easy and grateful to believe!"[1]

The *Inland Voyage* had been published in May, 1878, producing no more sensation than a small book, written for the sake of style by an unknown author, was likely to produce among the public, although the reviews showed uniform favour and occasional discernment. The author wrote to his mother: "I was more surprised at the tone of the critics than I suppose any one else. And the effect it has produced on me is one of shame. If they liked that so much, I ought to have given them something better, that's all. And I shall try to do so. Still it strikes me as odd; and I don't understand the vogue." And later in the year he has been reading it through again and finds it "not

[1] *Travels with a Donkey*, p. 310.

badly written, thin, mildly cheery and strained." His
final verdict, given in Samoa in the last year of his life,
was that though this book and the *Travels with a
Donkey* contained nothing but fresh air and a certain
style, they were good of their kind, and possessed a
simplicity of treatment which afterwards he thought
had passed out of his reach.

The first draft of the *Voyage* was made some time in
1877 in Edinburgh, much of it being taken without
alteration from his log-book. There are in this draft
numerous variations from the text as finally printed,
although many consecutive pages have no word altered, but the chief difference between them lies in the
fact that most of the longer passages of general reflections are not to be found in the draft. Thus in the
opening chapter the second and third and most of the
last paragraph are as yet wanting.

Of the work of the year, *Will o' the Mill* shows perhaps the greatest advance. It was the first of his tales
taken by the *Cornhill,* and in spite of the obvious influence of Hawthorne and a certain amount of dissatisfac-
tion with the uneven development of the allegory,
more than any of his shorter pieces, it produced the
impression that a new writer had arisen, original in his
conceptions, and already a master of style. The setting was composed, he told Mr. Iles, from a combina-
tion of the Murgthal in Baden and the Brenner Pass in
Tyrol, over which he went on his Grand Tour at the
age of twelve.

Apart from its manner, the interest of the story lies
for us in its divergence from Stevenson's scheme and
conduct of life. It was written, he told me, as an ex-

periment, in order to see what could be said in support
of the opposite theory: much as he used to present to
his cousin Bob any puzzling piece of action in order to
find out what could be urged in its defence.[1]   One of
his ruling maxims was that "Acts may be forgiven:
not even God can forgive the hanger-back"; yet here
he depicted the delight of fruition indefinitely deferred,
the prudence of giving no hostages to fortune, the
superiority of the man who suffices to himself.   In the
story, however, there were embodied so much wisdom,
so much spirit, so much courage, so much of all that
was best in the writer, that it imposed on others long
after it had ceased to satisfy himself.   And as a work
of art it may well outlast far more correct philosophy.
It has this also: although in later days he ventured on
a more elaborate treatment of his heroines, it seems to
me — if any man may venture so far — that it is impossible to maintain that he was still ignorant of the heart
of woman who now drew with so delicate and so firm
a touch the outlines of "the parson's Marjory."

The *Travels with a Donkey* were written in the winter and published in June, 1879.   In the spring Louis
wrote to R. A. M. Stevenson: "My book is through
the press.   It has good passages.   I can say no more.
A chapter called 'The Monks,' another 'A Camp in
the Dark,' a third 'A Night among the Pines.'   Each
of these has, I think, some stuff in it in the way of
writing.   But lots of it is mere protestations to F.,
most of which I think you will understand.   That is to
me the main thread of interest.   Whether the damned
public —   But that 's all one."

[1] *Memories and Portraits*, p. 187.

He returned to London and began to collaborate with Mr. Henley in a play based on the latest of his drafts of *Deacon Brodie,* which he had not touched since he was nineteen.   In the meantime he started on another walk, this time down the valley of the Stour, which separates the counties of Essex and Suffolk; but a sore heel soon brought him back to London, not unwillingly, as he found it "dull, cold, and not singularly pretty on the road."   In December he wrote to his mother: "I don't wish the play spoken of at all; for of course, as a first attempt, it will most likely come to nothing.   It is, however, pretty good in parts.   I work three hours every morning here in the club on the *brouillons;* and then three in the afternoon on the fair copy.   In bed by ten; here again in the morning, to the consternation of the servants, as soon as the club is open."

It was probably at this time that he made the social experiment recorded in *The Amateur Emigrant* of practising upon the public by "going abroad through a suburban part of London simply attired in a sleeve-waistcoat."

"The result was curious.   I then learned for the first time, and by the exhaustive process, how much attention ladies are accustomed to bestow on all male creatures of their own station; for, in my humble rig, each one who went by me caused a certain shock of surprise and a sense of something wanting.   In my normal circumstances, it appeared, every young lady must have paid me some passing tribute of a glance; and though I had often been unconscious of it when given, I was well aware of its absence when it was withheld.   My height seemed to decrease with every woman who passed me, for she passed me like a dog. This is one of my grounds for supposing that what are called the upper classes may sometimes produce a disagreeable impression in what are called the lower; and I wish some one would continue my experiment, and find out exactly at what stage of toilette a man becomes invisible to the well-regulated female eye." [1]

But life was not to be lived upon the old terms. His heart was elsewhere, and the news which reached him was disquieting. For some time it was fairly good; then Mrs. Osbourne fell seriously ill. There had been, there could be, no restoration of her home life; but it appeared that she would be able to obtain a divorce without causing any unnecessary distress to her family, and in this conjunction Stevenson could not see clearly what his course of action ought to be. He was first at Swanston with Mr. Henley, finishing *Deacon Brodie;* then in London; at Swanston again, this time alone, writing his chapters on *Lay Morals;* then at the Gareloch with his parents. In May he went to London, and, after staying with Mr. George Meredith, crossed over to France. Had he found a companion, he would perhaps have gone to the Pyrenees, but he spent most of his time at Cernay la Ville, and returned to London in the end of June. He there saw Mr. Macdonald of the *Times*, in reference to some negotiations for his employment; he expressed himself as unwilling to accept "leaders," but apparently asked for some more general commission, which, however, he did not receive.

The *Travels with a Donkey* had been published in June, and obtained the same unsubstantial success as

[1] *The Amateur Emigrant*, p. 83.

the *Inland Voyage*, although, contrary to its author's own judgment of the two books, it afterwards had slightly the better sale.

On 14th July he returned to Edinburgh, and by the 30th his mind was made up — to California he must go. From Edinburgh he came back to London, presumably to make arrangements for his start; and wherever he went, he found his friends unanimous in their opinion that he ought to stay at home. Under these circumstances it seemed to him so hopeless to expect any other judgment on the part of his parents, that he did not even go through the form of consulting them on the matter, and with open eyes went away, knowing that he need look for no further countenance from home. He had long felt it to be a duty that every man on reaching manhood should cease to be a burden to his father; he had now learned his craft, and every circumstance seemed to him to point out that the time was come for him to seek his own livelihood and justify his independence. These considerations were very present to his mind, and perhaps he hardly realised the distress which he would inevitably cause his parents by leaving them without a word and in almost total ignorance of the hopes and motives which inspired him.

CHAPTER VIII

" What a man truly wants, that will he get, or he will be changed in trying."— R. L. S., Aphorism.

" To My Wife

" Trusty, dusky, vivid, true,
　With eyes of gold and bramble-dew,
　Steel-true and blade-straight,
　The great artificer
　Made my mate.

" Honour, anger, valour, fire;
　A love that life could never tire,　.
　Death quench or evil stir,
　The mighty master
　Gave to her.

" Teacher, tender, comrade, wife,
　A fellow-farer true through life,
　Heart-whole and soul-free,
　The august father
　Gave to me."

Songs of Travel, No. xxvi.

From London he went north, and on August 7th, 1879, sailed from the Clyde in the steamship *Devonia*, bound for New York. She carried a number of emigrants, but Stevenson, though mixing freely with them, had, chiefly to obtain a table for his writing, taken his passage in the second cabin, which was almost indistinguishable from the steerage. His object in travelling in this fashion was, in the first instance, economy, and next to that, a desire to gain first-hand knowledge for himself of emigrants and emigration, which might be of immediate use for making a book and of ultimate service to him in a thousand ways. He suffered a good deal on the voyage, being already anxious and highly strung before he started, but he stuck manfully to his work and wrote, "in a slantindicular cabin, with the table playing bob-cherry with the ink-bottle," the greater part of *The Story of a Lie.* The rest of his time he devoted to making the acquaintance of his fellow-passengers, learning their histories, studying their characters, and—as any one may see between the lines of *The Amateur Emigrant*[1]—rendering them endless unobtrusive services, and helping and cheering them in every way possible. He passed easily for one of themselves. "Among my fellow-passengers," he wrote elsewhere,[2] "I passed generally as a mason, for the excellent reason that there was a mason on board who *happened to know;* and this fortunate event enabled me to mix with these working people on a footing of equality. . . . It chanced there was a blacksmith on board who was not only well mannered himself and a judge of manners, but a fellow besides of an original mind. He had early diagnosed me for a masquerader and a person out of place; and as we had grown intimate upon the voyage, I carried him my troubles. How did I behave? Was I, upon this crucial test, at all a gentleman? I might have asked eight hundred thousand blacksmiths (if Wales or the world contain so many) and they would

[1] *The Amateur Emigrant,* Edinburgh Edition.
[2] *Scribner's Magazine,* May, 1888.

have held my question for a mockery; but Jones was a man of genuine perception, thought a long time before he answered, looking at me comically, and reviewing (I could see) the events of the voyage, and then told me that 'on the whole' I did 'pretty well.' Mr. Jones was a humane man, and very much my friend, and he could get no further than 'on the whole' and 'pretty well.' I was chagrined at the moment for myself; on a larger basis of experience, I am now only concerned for my class. My coequals would have done but little better, and many of them worse."

The voyage passed without event, and the steamer arrived at New York on the evening of the 18th of August. Stevenson passed the night in a shilling Irish boarding-house. "A little Irish girl," he writes, "is now reading my book[1] aloud to her sister at my elbow; they chuckle, and I feel flattered. *P.S.*—Now they yawn, and I am indifferent: such a wisely conceived thing is vanity." The following day he spent in making purchases, and also is said to have entered the offices of various magazines to establish, if possible, an American connection. Angels have been dismissed unawares at other places and at other times, and—if there be any truth in the story—Stevenson found that the moment of his welcome was not yet come.

Within four-and-twenty hours of his first arrival he was already on his way as an emigrant to the Far West, a chief part of his baggage being "Bancroft's *History of the United States* in six fat volumes."

The railway journey began in floods of rain and the maximum of discomfort. The record of it is in the

[1] *I.e.* the *Travels with a Donkey*, then recently published.

hands of all to read, and I need say only that it occupied from a Monday evening to the Saturday morning of the following week, and that the tedium and stress of the last few days in the emigrant train proper were almost unbearable.

On the 30th of August Stevenson reached San Francisco, but so much had the long journey shaken him that he looked like a man at death's door. The news so far was good; Mrs. Osbourne was better, but that was all. To recover from the effects of his hardships he forthwith went another hundred and fifty miles to the south, and camped out by himself in the Coast Range of mountains beyond Monterey. But he had overtaxed his strength, and broke down. Two nights he " lay out under a tree in a sort of stupor," and if two frontiersmen in charge of a goat-ranche had not taken him in and tended him, there would have been an end of his story. They took him back to the ranche, and amid romantic surroundings and in that enchanting climate, he made a recovery for the time.

" I am now lying in an upper chamber, with a clinking of goat bells in my ears, which proves to me that the goats are come home and it will soon be time to eat. The old bear-hunter is doubtless now infusing tea; and Tom the Indian will come in with his gun in a few minutes."

Here he spent a couple of weeks, passing the mornings in teaching the children to read, and then went down to Monterey, where he remained until the middle of December. In those days it still was a small Mexican town, altered but slightly by the extraordinarily cosmopolitan character of the few strangers who visited it. In his own words, it was "a place of two or three streets, economically paved with sea-sand, and two or three lanes, which were watercourses in the rainy season, and at all times were rent up by fissures four or five feet deep. There were no street lights. . . . The houses were for the most part built of unbaked adobe brick, many of them old for so new a country, some of very elegant proportions, with low, spacious, shapely rooms, and walls so thick that the heat of summer never dried them to the heart. . . . There was no activity but in and around the saloons, where people sat almost all day long playing cards. . . . The smallest excursion was made on horseback. You would scarcely ever see the main street without a horse or two tied to posts, and making a fine figure with their Mexican housings. . . . In a place so exclusively Mexican as Monterey, you saw not only Mexican saddles, but true Vaquero riding—men always at the hand-gallop, up hill and down dale, and round the sharpest corner, urging their horses with cries and gesticulations and cruel rotatory spurs, checking them dead with a touch, or wheeling them right-about-face in a square yard. . . . Spanish was the language of the streets. It was difficult to get along without a word or two of that language for an occasion. The only communications in which the population joined were with a view to amusement. A weekly public ball took place with great etiquette, in addition to the numerous fandangoes in private houses. There was a really fair amateur brass band. Night after night, serenaders would be going about the street, sometimes in a company and with several instruments and voices together, sometimes severally, each guitar before a different window. It was a strange thing to lie awake in nineteenth-century America, and hear the guitar accompany, and one of these old, heart-breaking Spanish love-songs mount into the night air, perhaps in a deep baritone, perhaps in that high-pitched, pathetic, womanish alto which is so common among Mexican men, and which strikes on the unaccustomed ear as something not entirely human, but altogether sad." [1]

Here Stevenson found quarters curiously to his taste, which was simple, though discriminating. He lodged with the doctor, and for his meals went to a restaurant.

"Of all my private collection of remembered inns and restaurants—and I believe it, other things being equal, to be unrivalled—one particular house of entertainment stands forth alone. I am grateful, indeed, to many a swinging signboard, to many a rusty wine-bush; but not with the same kind of gratitude. Some were beautifully situated, some had an admirable table, some were the gathering-places of excellent companions; but take them for all in all, not one can be compared with Simoneau's at Monterey.

"To the front, it was part barber's shop, part bar; to the back, there was a kitchen and a *salle à manger*. The intending diner found himself in a little, chill, bare, adobe room, furnished with chairs and tables, and adorned with some oil sketches roughly brushed upon the wall in the manner of Barbizon and Cernay. The table, at whatever hour you entered, was already laid with a not spotless napkin, and, by way of epergne, with a dish of green peppers and tomatoes, pleasing alike to eye and palate. If you stayed there to meditate before a meal, you would hear Simoneau all about the kitchen, and rattling among the dishes."

The fragment breaks off, or we should have had a picture of M. Simoneau, the proprietor, with whom Stevenson "played chess and discussed the universe" daily. At his table there "sat down, day after day, a Frenchman, two Portuguese, an Italian, a Mexican, and a Scotsman; they had for common visitors an American from Illinois, a nearly pure-blood Indian woman, and a naturalised Chinese; and from time to time a Switzer and a German came down from country ranches for the night."

This society afforded Stevenson most of the diversion that he could now spare the time to enjoy. Of his adventures in the forest he has told us, and chiefly of that day when, setting fire to a tree in mere experiment and idleness of mind, he ran for his life in fear of being lynched. But during all these weeks he was working as he had hardly worked before. Half of a novel called *A Vendetta in the West* was written, and the whole of *The Pavilion on the Links*, which he had begun in London, was despatched to England. The scenery of the latter was, I believe, suggested by Dirleton in East Lothian, near North Berwick, and midway between Tantallon and Gillane, haunts of his boyhood, to which he returned in *Catriona*. At the same time he was writing up his emigrant experiences, about half of the original manuscript being completed at Monterey. There was a tiny local newspaper, *The Monterey Californian*, of which one of his friends was owner, editor, printer, and everything else, and to this Stevenson occasionally lent a hand. But he was still greatly agitated and worried, and though by this time word came from San Francisco that Mrs. Osbourne was well, and that matters were taking their course, the main object of his journey still seemed no nearer than before. The strain of exertion and anxiety was again too great, and " while leading a dull regular life in a mild climate," he developed pleurisy, and had for a few days to relax his exertions.

All this time he was the kindly and bright companion; his gaiety and courage never flagged. " There is something in me worth saying," he wrote to Mr. Henley, " though I can't find what it is just yet."

About the middle of December he came to San Francisco, and there hired the most economical lodging he could find, at all compatible with the conditions of his work—a single room in a poor house in Bush Street. All his meals he took outside at some of the cheap restaurants; in San Francisco it is probably easier to fare well at small expense than in any other city in America. He lived at seventy cents a day, and worked yet harder than before. He made inquiries about work on the San Francisco *Bulletin*, but the payment offered by that newspaper for literary articles, which were all he was ready to undertake, was too small to be of any use to a writer so painstaking and so deliberate. The *Bulletin* afterwards accepted at its own rates a couple of papers which he had not written specially for it, but considered unsuitable for any other purpose, but his connection with the San Francisco press was absolutely limited to this transaction.[1]

[1] There is no ground for the statement that Stevenson ever acted as reporter for the *Chronicle* or any other San Francisco paper. It is

But the worst part of the change from Monterey was that he was thrown more upon himself. In place of the bright social life of the little Spanish town, a life such as is common on the Continent of Europe, but is hardly to be found in England, he was plunged into the terrible solitude of a large city. On the 26th December he writes: " For four days I have spoken to no one but my landlady or landlord, or to restaurant waiters. This is not a gay way to pass Christmas, is it ? " And again: " After weeks in this city, I know only a few neighbouring streets; I seem to be cured of all my adventurous whims, and even of human curiosity, and am content to sit here by the fire and await the course of fortune."

It was in these days that he met that " bracing, Republican postman in the city of San Francisco. I lived in that city among working folk, and what my neighbours accepted at the postman's hands—nay, what I took from him myself—it is still distasteful to recall." [1]

His friends were very few, and those of but a few weeks' standing. They hardly extended, indeed, beyond Mr. Virgil Williams and his wife, the artist couple to whom *The Silverado Squatters* was afterwards dedicated, and Mr. Charles Warren Stoddard, whose picturesque lodging is commemorated in *The Wrecker*.

expressly contradicted by Mr. John P. Young, then and now managing editor of that journal, and his denial is borne out by the records of the paper and by the recollections of all who knew Stevenson in California at the time. A legend that the San Francisco doctors refused advice to the sick man except for ready money is equally unfounded.

[1] *Later Essays*, Edinburgh Edition, p. 291.

In Mr. Williams he found a man of great culture and refinement, a scholar as well as a painter, who was always ready to respond to his verses, and, together with his wife, able and eager to discuss the literatures of Europe. Their house was always open to Stevenson, and their only regret was that he could not come more frequently. To Mr. Stoddard also he was no less welcome a companion; from him he borrowed the delightful books of Herman Melville, *Typee* and *Omoo*, and the *South Sea Idylls*,[1] which charmed Stevenson alike with their subject and their style. So here in his darkest hour he received the second impulse, which in the end was to " cast him out as by a freshet" upon those " ultimate islands."

San Francisco itself was still far from a prosaic place; its early history and its large foreign population rendered it not less dangerous than picturesque. Kearney, the Irish demagogue, had only just " been snuffed out by Mr. Coleman, backed by his San Francisco Vigilantes and three Gatling guns." Stevenson himself was not without experiences, perhaps less uncommon there at that time than in other large cities. " There are rough quarters where it is dangerous o' nights; cellars of public entertainment which the wary pleasure-seeker chooses to avoid. Concealed weapons are unlawful, but the law is continually broken. One editor was shot dead while I was there; another walked the streets accompanied by a bravo, his guardian angel. I have been quietly eating a dish of oysters in a restaurant, where, not more than ten minutes after I had left, shots were

---

[1] Published in England by Messrs. Chatto & Windus in 1874 as *Summer Cruising in the South Seas*, by Charles Warren Stoddard.

exchanged and took effect; and one night, about ten o'clock, I saw a man standing watchfully at a street corner with a long Smith-and-Wesson glittering in his hand behind his back. Somebody had done something he should not, and was being looked for with a vengeance."[1]

But his private needs now pressed upon him; money was growing scarce; the funds he had brought with him were exhausted, and those transmitted from England, being partly his own money and partly the payment for his recent work, very frequently failed to reach him. In the end of January he had to drop from a fifty-cent to a twenty-five-cent dinner, and already had directed his friend Mr. Charles Baxter to dispose of his books in Edinburgh and to send him the proceeds.

His diligence had not been without results. *The Amateur Emigrant* had been finished and sent home; likewise two *Cornhill* articles on "Thoreau" and "Yoshida Torajiro." His interest in Japan was chiefly derived from his acquaintance with sundry Japanese who came to Edinburgh to study lighthouse engineering, with some of whom he afterwards for a while carried on correspondence.

The influence of America in literature during the nineteenth century has perhaps been most deeply exercised upon English authors through Hawthorne, Whitman, and Poe. Other names have been more widely celebrated, but these three have the most intimately affected their fellow-writers, and the influence of the two latter at any rate has been out of proportion to their achievement. With Stevenson Thoreau came after his country-

[1] *Pacific Capitals*, Edinburgh Edition, p. 198.

men in point of time, but the effect was even more considerable: "I have scarce written ten sentences, since I was introduced to Thoreau, but his influence might be somewhere detected by a close observer." Had Stevenson not now been on the threshold of marriage, he might yet more strongly have been affected by these ascetic and self-sufficing doctrines.

At this time *Prince Otto* began to suffer a resurrection out of one of his old plays, *Semiramis, a Tragedy*, but as yet it was known as *The Greenwood State, a Romance*. An article on Benjamin Franklin and the Art of Virtue was projected, and another upon William Penn, whose *Fruits of Solitude* now became a very favourite book with Stevenson. "A Dialogue between Two Puppets"[1] was also written, and about the half of an autobiography in five books.[2]

His prospects were gloomy; for although the manuscripts he had sent home were accepted by editors, yet the judgment of his friends upon some of them was justly unfavourable, and at this crisis he could not afford rejection or even delay in payment.

His correspondence with his parents since his departure had been brief and unsatisfactory. His father, being imperfectly informed as to his motives and plans, naturally took that dark view of his son's conduct to which his temperament predisposed him. But even so, hearing of Louis' earlier illness, he sent him a twenty-pound note, though, as fate would have it, this was one of the letters that miscarried.

Lonely, ill, and poor; estranged from his people, unsuccessful in his work, and discouraged in his attempt

[1] *Miscellanea*, p. 28.   [2] See pp. 99, 102.

to maintain himself, Stevenson yet did not lose heart or go back for one moment from his resolution. He wrote to Mr. Baxter: " *20th Jan.*—I lead a pretty happy life, though you might not think it. I have great fun trying to be economical, which I find as good a game of play as any other. I have no want of occupation, and though I rarely see any one to speak to, have little time to weary."

"However ill he might be," says Mrs. Williams, "or however anxious had been his vigils, he was always gay, eloquent, and boyish, with the peculiar youthfulness of spirit that was destined to last him to the end."

He stuck to his work; even, a harder feat, he had the determination to give himself a week's holiday. But though his spirit was indomitable, his physical powers were exhausted; his landlady's small child was very ill, and he sat up nursing it. The child recovered, but Stevenson a short while afterwards broke down, and could go on no more.

He was, as he afterwards wrote to Mr. Gosse, on the verge of a galloping consumption, subject to cold sweats, prostrating attacks of cough, sinking fits in which he lost the power of speech, fever, and all the ugliest circumstances of the disease.[1]

Fortunately by this date his future wife had obtained her divorce, and was at liberty to give him as nurse those services for which there was unfortunately only too frequent occasion during the next few years. It was a very anxious time, and he was nearer " the grey ferry " than he had been since childhood. Slowly he mended, and his recovery was helped by his letters and

[1] *Letters*, i. 169.

telegrams from home. Already by the middle of February he must have heard that his father admitted that the case was not what he supposed, and that if there were as long a delay as possible, he was prepared to do his best in the matter. At that very date Mr. Stevenson was writing again that it was preposterous of Louis to scrimp himself, and that if he would inform him what money he wanted, it would be sent by telegram, if required. And early in April a telegram came, announcing to Louis that in future he might count upon two hundred and fifty pounds a year. His gratitude was unbounded; he realised very clearly what his extremity had been and the fate from which he had been rescued.

To Mr. Baxter again he wrote:—

"It was a considerable shock to my pride to break down; but there—it's done, and cannot be helped. Had my health held out another month, I should have made a year's income; but breaking down when I did, I am surrounded by unfinished works. It is a good thing my father was on the spot, or I should have had to work and die."

All obstacles were at last removed, and on May 19th, 1880, Robert Louis Stevenson was married to Fanny Van de Grift at San Francisco, in the house of the Rev. Dr. Scott, no one else but Mrs. Scott and Mrs. Williams being present.

Of the marriage it need only be said that from the beginning to the end husband and wife were all in all to one another. His friends rejoiced to find in her, as Mr. Colvin says, "a character as strong, interesting, and romantic almost as his own; an inseparable sharer of all his thoughts, and staunch companion of all his adventures; the most open-hearted of friends to all who loved him; the most shrewd and stimulating critic of his work; and in sickness, despite her own precarious health, the most devoted and most efficient of nurses." [1]

Two years before his death Stevenson wrote, in reference to another love-match: " To be sure it is always annoying when people choose their own wives; and I know only one form of consolation—they know best what they want. As I look back, I think my marriage was the best move I ever made in my life. Not only would I do it again; I cannot conceive the idea of doing otherwise."

Of his devotion to his wife he was even more reticent than of his affection to his parents. " I love my wife," he once wrote, "I do not know how much, nor can, nor shall, unless I lost her." And once or twice in letters to those who knew and loved them best, he almost unconsciously revealed his affection, which, for the rest, is embodied in the lyric written a year or two before his death, and printed at the head of this chapter. As he lived, so he died, and the last moments of his consciousness were occupied with the attempt to lift the burden of foreboding which was weighing so heavily upon his wife.

Immediately after the marriage Stevenson and his wife and stepson went to the country fifty miles north of San Francisco, there to seek health in the mountains. How they took possession of all that was left of a mining-town, and lived in isolation and independence among the ruins, is told once for all in *The Silverado*

[1] *Letters*, i. 179.

Squatters; but it is not mentioned that Mrs. Stevenson and her son there sickened of diphtheria, and that the anxiety and danger of a serious illness were added to their lot.

By this time Stevenson knew that his father and mother were longing for nothing in the world so much as to see his face again, to make the acquaintance of his wife, and to welcome her for his sake.

It was not, however, until July was well advanced that the party could leave Calistoga, but on the 7th of August they sailed from New York, and ten days later they found Thomas Stevenson and his wife and Sidney Colvin waiting for them at Liverpool.

In California the year before, Louis had written of his father: "Since I have gone away, I have found out for the first time how I love that man; he is dearer to me than all, except Fanny." And now his joy at seeing his parents was heightened, if possible, by the share which his wife had in their reception. Any doubts that had existed as to the wisdom of his choice were soon driven from their minds, and the new-comer was received into their affection with as much readiness and cordiality as if it were they and not Louis who had made the match. Old Mr. Stevenson in particular discovered in his daughter-in-law so many points which she possessed in common with himself, that his natural liking passed rapidly into an appreciation and affection such as are usually the result only of years of intimacy. In his own wife's notes I find that before his death he made his son promise that he would " never publish anything without Fanny's approval."

In consequence of the new order of things, Swanston

Cottage had finally been given up early in the summer, and the family party, passing hastily through Edinburgh, went on first to Blair Athol and then to Strathpeffer, returning to Heriot Row in the middle of September. Never before, Stevenson declared, had he appreciated the beauty of the Highlands, but now he was all enthusiasm. Except an article at Calistoga, he had done no work for months, but these new influences suffered him to rest no longer: he wrote " The Scotsman's Return from Abroad,"[1] and was planning for himself no less a book on Scotland than a *History of the Union*. At Strathpeffer he met Principal Tulloch, already a friend of his parents and the editor of *Fraser's Magazine*, with whom he had much talk, and by whom he was confirmed in the purpose of his book. Moreover, "The Scotsman's Return" and the paper on Monterey were accepted for *Fraser*.

On the other hand, both Stevenson and his father now considered it undesirable to publish the account of his recent experiences as an emigrant in its existing form. It was necessarily somewhat personal, and the circumstances under which it was written had told against its success. It had been sold, but it was the work which his friends had criticised most severely, and there no longer existed the dire need for making money by any possible means. The sum paid by the publishers was refunded by Mr. Stevenson, and for the time being the book was withdrawn.

The exile's return to his native country was of short duration, for the hardships he had endured and his consequent illness had rendered him quite unable to face a

1 *Underwoods*, xii.: In Scots.

Scottish winter. On consulting his uncle, Dr. George Balfour, the well-known Edinburgh doctor, he was informed of his condition, and advised to try the climate of the High Alps, which had lately come into favour as a resort for patients suffering from phthisis.

Accordingly, on October 7th Stevenson left Edinburgh with his wife and stepson and a new member of the family, who held a high place in their affections, and was an important element in all their arrangements for the next half-dozen years. This was a black Skye terrier, a present from Sir Walter Simpson, after whom he was called, until "Wattie" had passed into "Woggs," and finally became unrecognisable as "Bogue." In Heriot Row every dog worshipped Thomas Stevenson (with the sole exception of "Jura," who was alienated by jealousy), and so Louis never had a dog until now who really regarded him as owner. But Woggs was a person of great character, with views and a temper of his own, entirely devoted to his master and mistress, and at odds with the world at large.

In London, Dr. Andrew Clark confirmed both the opinion and the advice which had been given, and a few days only were spent in seeing Stevenson's friends, who now found their first opportunity to welcome him back and to make the acquaintance of his wife.

CHAPTER IX

" A mountain valley, an Alpine winter, and an invalid's weakness
make up among them a prison of the most effective kind."
R. L. S., *Pall Mall Gazette*, 21st February, 1881.

By the middle of October the party again started,
made a journey broken by frequent halts, and on the
4th of November reached Davos Platz, where they
were to spend the winter. They took up their quarters
in the Hotel Belvedere, the nucleus of the present large
establishment, and there they stayed until the following
April.

The great feature of the place for Stevenson was the
presence of John Addington Symonds, who, having
come there three years before on his way to Egypt, had
taken up his abode in Davos, and was now building
himself a house. To him the newcomer bore a letter of
introduction from Mr. Gosse. On November 5th Louis
wrote to his mother: "We got to Davos last evening;
and I feel sure we shall like it greatly. I saw Symonds
this morning, and already like him; it is such sport to
have a literary man around. My father can understand
me, when he thinks what it would be to come up here
for a winter and find Tait.[1] Symonds is like a Tait to
me; eternal interest in the same topics, eternal cross-

[1] Professor P. G. Tait, the eminent man of science, Professor of
Natural Philosophy in the University of Edinburgh, 1860-1900: a close
friend of Thomas Stevenson.

causewaying of special knowledge.   That makes hours to fly."   And a little later he wrote: "Beyond its splendid climate, Davos has but one advantage — the neighbourhood of J. A. Symonds.   I daresay you know his work, but the man is far more interesting." [1]

This first winter Stevenson produced but little.   He arrived full of eagerness to begin his Scottish history, but a little study and reflection, following upon his new-found enthusiasm for the parts of Scotland where he had been staying, had fixed his attention exclusively upon one section of his original subject, and for the time he limited his view to a history of the Highlands extending from 1715 to his own day.   "I breathe after this Highland business," he wrote in December, "feeling a real, fresh, lively, and modern subject, full of romance and scientific interest, in front of me.   It is likely it will turn into a long essay."

Even this, it seemed, was beyond his powers for the present.   The doctor in a few weeks spoke hopefully of his case, but the climate, though beneficial in the long run, was not at first conducive to any deliberate effort. Of the sensations produced in himself, Stevenson has left an analysis that may be contrasted with the moods of the convalescent in "Ordered South."

". . . In many ways it is a trying business to reside upon the Alps.[2] . . . But one thing is undeniable — that in the rare air, clear, cold, and blinding light of Alpine winters, a man takes a certain troubled delight in his existence, which can nowhere else be paralleled. He is perhaps no happier, but he is stingingly alive.   It

[1] *Dictionary of National Biography*, sub. "Symonds."

[2] *Pall Mall Gazette*, 5th March, 1881, " The Stimulation of the Alps."

does not, perhaps, come out of him in work or exercise, yet he feels an enthusiasm of the blood unknown in more temperate climates. It may not be health, but it is fun.

"There is nothing more difficult to communicate on paper than this baseless ardour, this stimulation of the brain, this sterile joyousness of spirits. You wake every morning, see the gold upon the snow-peaks, become filled with courage, and bless God for your prolonged existence. The valleys are but a stride to you; you cast your shoe over the hill-tops; your ears and your heart sing; in the words of an unverified quotation from the Scotch psalms, you feel yourself fit 'on the wings of all the winds' to 'come flying all abroad.' Europe and your mind are too narrow for that flood of energy. Yet it is notable that you are hard to root out of your bed; that you start forth singing, indeed, on your walk, yet are unusually ready to turn home again; that the best of you is volatile; and that although the restlessness remains till night, the strength is early at an end. With all these heady jollities, you are half conscious of an underlying languor in the body; you prove not to be so well as you had fancied; you weary before you have well begun; and though you mount at morning with the lark, that is not precisely a songbird's heart that you bring back with you when you return with aching limbs and peevish temper to your inn.

"It is hard to say wherein it lies, but this joy of Alpine winters is its own reward. Baseless, in a sense, it is more than worth more permanent improvements. The dream of health is prefect while it lasts; and if, in

trying to realise it, you speedily wear out the dear hallu-
cination, still every day, and many times a day, you are
conscious of a strength you scarce possess, and a delight
in living as merry as it proves to be transient. The
brightness — heaven and earth conspiring to be bright;
the levity and quiet of the air; the odd, stirring
silence — more stirring than a tumult; the snow, the
frost, the enchanted landscape: all have their part in
the effect on the memory, *tous vous tapent sur la tête;*
and yet when you have enumerated all, you have gone
no nearer to explain or even to qualify the delicate exhilaration that you feel — delicate, you may say, and yet
excessive, greater than can be said in prose, almost
greater than an invalid can bear. There is a certain
wine of France, known in England in some gaseous disguise, but when drunk in the land of its nativity, still
as a pool, clean as river water, and as heady as verse.
It is more than probable that in its noble natural condition this was the very wine of Anjou so beloved
by Athos in the *Musketeers.* Now if the reader has
ever washed down a liberal second breakfast with the
wine in question, and gone forth, on the back of these
dilutions, into a sultry, sparkling noontide, he will
have felt an influence almost as genial, although
strangely grosser, than this fairy titillation of the nerves
among the snow and sunshine of the Alps. That also
is a mode, we need not say of intoxication, but of in-
sobriety. Thus also a man walks in a strong sunshine
of the mind, and follows smiling, insubstantial meditations. And, whether he be really so clever or so strong
as he supposes, in either case he will enjoy his chimæra
while it lasts.

"The influence of this giddy air displays itself in many secondary ways. People utter their judgments with a cannonade of syllables; a big word is as good as a meal to them; and the turn of a phrase goes further than humour or wisdom. By the professional writer many sad vicissitudes have to be undergone. At first, he cannot write at all. The heart, it appears, is unequal to the pressure of business, and the brain, left without nourishment, goes into a mild decline. Next, some power of work returns to him, accompanied by jumping headaches. Last, the spring is opened, and there pours at once from his pen a world of blatant, hustling polysyllables. He writes them in good faith and with a sense of inspiration; it is only when he comes to read what he has written that surprise and disquiet seize upon his mind. What is he to do, poor man? All his little fishes talk like whales. This yeasty inflation, this stiff and strutting architecture of the sentence, have come upon him while he slept; and it is not he, it is the Alps who are to blame. He is not, perhaps, alone, which somewhat comforts him. Nor is the ill without a remedy. Some day, when the spring returns, he shall go down a little lower in this world, and remember quieter inflections and more modest language. . . .

"Is it a return of youth, or is it a congestion of the brain? It is a sort of congestion, perhaps, that leads the invalid, when all goes well, to face the new day with such a bubbling cheerfulness. It is certainly congestion that makes night hideous with visions; all the chambers of a many-storeyed caravanserai haunted with vociferous nightmares, and many wakeful people

217

come down late for breakfast in the morning. Upon that theory the cynic may explain the whole affair — exhilaration, nightmares, pomp of tongue, and all. But on the other hand, the peculiar blessedness of boyhood may itself be but a symptom of the same complaint, for the two effects are strangely similar; and the frame of mind of the invalid upon the Alps is a sort of intermittent youth, with periods of lassitude. The fountain of Juventus does not play steadily in these parts; but there it plays, and possibly nowhere else."

Apart from this exhilaration, there was much that he disliked in Davos, more especially the cut-and-dry walks alone possible to him, the monotonous river, the snow (in which he could see no colour), and the confinement to a single valley. "The mountains are about you like a trap," he wrote; "you cannot foot it up a hillside and behold the sea as a great plain, but live in holes and corners, and can change only one for the other."

The drawbacks of hotel life seem to have affected him but little; he had the company of his wife, and a constant interest in his stepson, who, having brought the toy-press given him the previous spring in California and used at Silverado, now devoted to printing all the time he could secure from lessons with his tutor.

A characteristic story which I have from Mrs. Stevenson belongs to this period. When they were leaving for Davos, her father-in-law, warned by the experiences of Louis in California, made her promise that she would let him know if at any time they were in want of money.

"The time came," she says, "when Louis had influenza and did need more, but he would not let me tell his father. I used every argument. At last I said, 'What do you think should be done with the money your father has so carefully laid by for the use of his family?' 'It should be given,' said Louis, 'to some young man of talent, who is in poor health and could not otherwise afford to get a necessary change of climate.' 'Oh, very well,' said I, 'I shall appeal to your father at once in the case of a young man named Stevenson, who is in just that position.' At this Louis could only laugh, and I wrote the story to his father, who was much amused by it, and of course sent the necessary supplies."

In these days, and indeed throughout his life, he was often unreasonable, but this very unreason seems always to have had a quality and a charm of its own, which only endeared Stevenson the more to those who suffered under its caprice, as two other anecdotes of Davos may serve to show. A young Church of England parson, who knew him but slightly, was roused one morning about six o'clock by a message that Stevenson wanted to see him immediately. Knowing how ill his friend was, he threw on his clothes and rushed to Stevenson's room, only to see a haggard face gazing from the bed-clothes, and to hear an agonised voice say, "For God's sake, ——, have you got a Horace?"

Another friend had received from Italy a present of some Christmas roses, to which particular associations gave a personal sentiment and value. Stevenson was seeking high and low for some flowers—the occasion, I think, was the birthday of a girl who could never live to see another—he heard of the arrival of these. He came, he stated the paramount necessity of depriving his friend, and he bore the flowers away. The two stories might end here, and show Stevenson in rather an unamiable light: their point is that neither of his friends ever dreamed of resenting his conduct or regarding it with any other feeling but affectionate amusement.

Often in the evening he would turn into the billiard-room, and there his talk might be heard at its best. A fellow-visitor has given a spirited and sympathetic description of him in those days, and adds: "Once only do I remember seeing him play a game of billiards, and a truly remarkable performance it was. He played with all the fire and dramatic intensity that he was apt to put into things. The balls flew wildly about, on or off the table as the case might be, but seldom indeed ever threatened a pocket or got within a hand's-breadth of a cannon. 'What a fine thing a game of billiards is,' he remarked to the astonished onlookers, '—once a year or so!'"[1]

When he was well, Stevenson had to be out of doors a good deal, and spent the time mostly in walks, often with his dog for a companion.

"*15th December, 1880.*— MY DEAR MOTHER,—I shall tell you about this morning. When I got out with Woggs about half-past seven, the sky was low and grey; the Tinzenhorn and the other high peaks were covered. It had snowed all night, a fine, soft snow; and all the ground had a gloss, almost a burnish, from the new coating. The woods were elaborately pow-

[1] Mr. Harold Vallings in *Temple Bar*, February, 1901, p. 25.

dered grey—not a needle but must have had a crystal. In the road immediately below me, a long train of sack-laden sledges was going by, drawn by four horses, with an indescribable smoothness of motion, and no sound save that of the bells. On the other road, across the river, four or five empty sledges were returning towards Platz, some of the drivers sitting down, some standing up in their vehicles; they glided forward without a jolt or a tremor, not like anything real, but like cardboard figures on a toy-theatre. I wonder if you can understand how odd this looked."

Occasionally he joined in skating and more frequently in the tobogganing then newly introduced. The latter experiences, as in all sports in which he ever took part, were delightful to him chiefly for the surroundings, and quite apart from all rivalry or competition, since, as he says in the *Inland Voyage*, he " held all racing as a creature of the devil." The following passage shows how he extracted the keenest pleasure both from the exercise itself and the romantic conditions with which he was able to invest it:—

" Perhaps the true way to toboggan is alone and at night. First comes the tedious climb, dragging your instrument behind you. Next a long breathing-space, alone with snow and pine woods, cold, silent, and solemn to the heart. Then you push off; the toboggan fetches way; she begins to feel the hill, to glide, to swim, to gallop. In a breath you are out from under the pine-trees, and a whole heaven full of stars reels and flashes overhead. Then comes a vicious effort; for by this time your wooden steed is speeding like the wind, and you are spinning round a corner, and the whole glittering valley and all the lights in all the great hotels lie for a moment at your feet; and the next you are racing once more in the shadow of the night, with close-shut teeth and beating heart. Yet a little while and you will be landed on the highroad by the door of your own hotel. This, in an atmosphere tingling with forty degrees of frost, in a night made luminous with stars and snow, and girt with strange white mountains, teaches the pulse an unaccustomed tune, and adds a new excitement to the life of man upon his planet." [1]

In the meanwhile he was allowed to work two hours in the morning, and one, if he wished, in the afternoon, and this time was not wholly without result. The first edition of *Virginibus Puerisque* — his earliest volume of collected papers — was prepared for the press, and the second essay in that book and the thrice-rejected article on Raeburn were there printed for the first time. The essay on Pepys was written, and a paper for the *Fortnightly*, but this was all the prose that he succeeded in finishing before his departure, except the four articles on Davos, which appeared in the *Pall Mall Gazette*. The last were mere impressions, anonymous, unfinished, and unrevised: yet no one can doubt for a moment the authorship of the extracts I have given.

Chiefly for his own amusement during the winter, he wrote also a good deal of familiar verse, the best of which was in Scots dialect, and included the lines addressed to the author of *Rab and his Friends*. In a series of octo-syllabic stanzas he denounced certain dishonest tradesmen

[1] " Alpine Diversions," *Pall Mall Gazette*, 26th February, 1881.

of Davos, and he also wrote a sequence of sonnets — almost his only use of this metrical form — their subject being one Peter Brash, a publican of Edinburgh, who had been the subject of his early jokes.

An outline of the Highland history may be found in the *Letters*,[1] but the book itself remained unwritten, and is never likely now to become what Stevenson could have made of it. But he spent some time in preparatory reading, and even began to learn Gaelic for the purpose, though he never got beyond the rudiments of the language.

A health-resort, from its very conditions, often casts upon a visitor shadows of death and bereavement, but this year the Stevensons were affected with the deepest sympathy for a loss that touched them nearly: their friend Mrs. Sitwell arrived unexpectedly with her son, who was already in the last stages of a swift consumption, and before the end came in April, there were but the alternations of despair and of hoping against hope until the blow fell.

Shortly afterwards Stevenson and his wife set out for France, accompanied only by Woggs, for the boy had gone to England to school. They spent several weeks, first at Barbizon; then in Paris, whence they were driven by drains; and at St. Germain, where Stevenson for the first time in his life heard a nightingale sing, and, having proclaimed that no sounds in nature could equal his favourite blackbird, forthwith surrendered all prejudice and fell into an ecstasy. They found themselves in straits at St. Germain, owing to the failure of supplies and the general suspicious appearance of Stevenson's

[1] *Letters*, i. 187.

wardrobe; being suddenly delivered from insults, they left their landlord, as Mrs. Stevenson alleged, in the belief that he had turned from his doors the eccentric son of a wealthy English nobleman.

They reached Edinburgh May 30th, 1881, and three days later started with his mother for Pitlochry, where they spent two months at Kinnaird Cottage; his father coming to them as often as business permitted. Louis had written to his parents that for country quarters his desiderata were these: "A house, not an inn, at least not an hotel; a burn within reach; heather and a fir or two. If these can be combined, I shall be pretty happy." These requisites he found, and indeed the man would be hard to satisfy who asked more of any stream— "a little green glen with a burn, a wonderful burn, gold and green and snow-white, singing loud and low in different steps of its career, now pouring over miniature crags, now fretting itself to death in a maze of rocky stairs and pots; never was so sweet a little river. Behind, great purple moorlands reaching to Ben Vrackie."[1]

He had thus his heart's desire, and in return, if (as he was always urging) man is but a steward on parole, he did not fail to repay mankind for this season of delight. For in these two months he wrote "Thrawn Janet" and "The Merry Men." "The Body Snatcher" belongs to the same time, all three being intended for a volume of tales of the supernatural. For "Thrawn Janet" Stevenson afterwards claimed that if he had never written anything but this tale and the story of "Tod Lapraik" in *Catriona*, he would yet have been a writer.[2] It was

[1] *Letters*, i. 204.
[2] *Vailima Letters*, p. 241.

the outcome of a study of the Scotch literature of witch-craft, and is hardly open to any other criticism than that which its author himself found against it. " 'Thrawn Janet' has two defects; it is true only historically, true for a hill parish in Scotland in old days, not true for man-kind and the world. Poor Mr. Soulis' faults we may eagerly recognise as virtues, and we feel that by his con-version he was merely worsened; and this, although the story carries me away every time I read it, leaves a painful impression on my mind." Even from the days of the *Edinburgh University Magazine* he had attached great importance to the names of his characters, and was never weary of improvising new lists for his amuse-ment. "My own uncle," he wrote to Mr. Barrie, "has simply the finest name in the world, *Ramsay Traquair*. Beat that you cannot." But I can remember his saying to me one day with a tone of deep regret, "I have al-ready used up the best name in all the world — Mr. Soulis."

"The Merry Men" was always one of his favourites, rather on account of the sentiment and the style than for the actual story. It was, as he put it, "a fantasia, or vision of the sea," and was designed to express the feeling of the west coast of Scotland as he conceived it in accordance with the memories of his engineering days, especially the weeks spent upon the island of Earraid.

He had now found his powers in dialect, in which hitherto he had written only a few verses and recorded but a few remembered phrases in his sketches or essays. But from this time much of the speech of his strongest novels was in Scotch, more or less broad, and the fame of Stevenson as a novelist is inseparably connected with his mastery over the common tongue of his own country. It may, perhaps, be added that the work done at Pitlochry is the only published prose that he ever wrote in the vernacular in Scotland itself. [1]

Over and above these stories he had in his mind at this time a scheme in connection with Jean Cavalier, the Protestant leader of the Cévennes in the eighteenth century, who had been a favourite hero with him since his travels with the donkey in that region. A copy of verses on Cavalier survives in one of his notebooks, but in spite of the inquiries he made of Mr. Gosse and others upon the subject, he seems never to have touched it again.

Towards the end of June he heard that Professor Æneas Mackay was about to resign the chair of History and Constitutional Law in the University of Edinburgh. It was possible to discharge the duties of this professorship by lecturing only during the summer session; the election was in the hands of the Faculty of Advocates, and Stevenson resolved to stand. Of the history of Scotland he knew more at any rate than some who had formerly held the chair: his knowledge of Constitutional Law was probably limited to what he had learned during one session from an infrequent attendance at the lectures of the professor, which were confined to the subject of Constitutional History with special reference

---

[1] Here is a picture from one of his notebooks. Could any other language have produced just the same effect? —

" The gloaming had come lang syne; there was a wee red winter sun on the ae side, and on the ither a cauld, wameless moon; the snaw in the lang loan squeaked under my feet as I ran."

to England; and to this topic I doubt whether Stevenson had ever given any serious attention whatever. He applied to his friends and got together a set of thirteen testimonials that are a tribute to the ingenuity of the human intellect, and were wholly disregarded by the electors. Grateful as Louis was to the loyalty of his supporters, he did not fail to see the humour of their conjunction: "It is an odd list of names. Church of England, Church of Scotland, Free Kirk, Pessimist, Radical, Tory: certainly I am not a party man." In the meantime he was so full of the idea, and so eager to try his powers, that he used to deliver specimen lectures to his stepson. The boy was seated on a chair, while the would-be professor declaimed for an hour upon Constitutional History, every now and then stopping to make sure that his class was following his meaning. The election took place in the winter, and Stevenson, although disappointed, was not surprised at the completeness of his failure.

On August 2nd the party left for Braemar; on the journey, Stevenson first conceived the family of Durrisdeer and the earlier part of *The Master of Ballantrae*, though both as yet were nameless, and it was six years and more before he began to set any word of it on paper.

At Braemar, having more accommodation, they were able to enjoy the society of some of their friends — Mr. Colvin, Mr. Baxter, and others. One of the first who arrived was Dr. Alexander Hay Japp, a new acquaintance, invited to discuss Thoreau, and to set Stevenson right upon one or two points in his history. Thoreau was duly discussed, but before the visitor left, he heard

the first eight or ten chapters of *Treasure Island,* then
newly written, and carried off the fair copy of the
manuscript, as far as it went, that he might offer it to
a publisher. Stevenson himself has told the history of
the book, his first book of which the public ever heard,
in one of those articles of reminiscence condemned by
his critics as premature, that now seem only too few
and too short for all of us. Having first drawn the
chart of an island (charts being to him "of all books
the least wearisome to read and the richest in matter"),
he then from the names, marked at random, constructed
a story in order to please his schoolboy stepson (who
had asked him to try and write "something interesting"); his father, another schoolboy in disguise, took
fire at this and urged him on, helping him with lists
and suggestions; unconscious memory came to his aid,
and *Treasure Island* was half written.[1]

Mr. Gosse immediately succeeded Dr. Japp as the
family visitor, and under his congenial influence the
story, which at first was called *The Sea Cook,* grew at
the rate of a chapter a day; before Stevenson left
Braemar, nineteen chapters had been written.[2] As
soon as the idea of publication occurred, the book had
been intended for Messrs. Routledge, but by Dr. Japp's
good offices it was accepted for *Young Folks* by Mr.
Henderson, the proprietor, when he saw the opening
chapters and heard an outline of the story.

In this summer Stevenson first began to write the

[1] " My First Book," *Juvenilia,* p. 288.

[2] I am greatly obliged both to Mr. Gosse and to Dr. Japp for their
recollections of this time. See also the *Academy,* lviii. pp. 189, 209,
237.

verses for children, which were afterwards published in the *Child's Garden.* His mother tells how she had Miss Kate Greenaway's *Birthday Book for Children,* with verses by Mrs. Sale Barker, then newly published, and how Louis took it up one day, and saying, "These are rather nice rhymes, and I don't think they would be difficult to do," proceeded to try his hand. About fourteen numbers seem to have been written in the Highlands, and apparently after three more had been added, they were then discontinued for a time.

But in the meanwhile the weather grew suddenly bad; Stevenson made a hurried flight (in a respirator) from Braemar on September 23rd, and after a few days in Edinburgh, passed on to London. Here he called on his new publisher; "a very amusing visit indeed; ordered away by the clerks, who refused loudly to believe I had any business; and at last received most kindly by Mr. Henderson."

From London they passed to Paris and so to Davos, which they reached on October 18th. This year they had taken for the winter a châlet belonging to the Hôtel Buol, where Symonds was still living; they hired a servant of their own, and only occasionally took meals in the hotel.

This winter differed considerably from the last. Stevenson was in better health, and being accustomed to the climate, and also less subject to interruption, produced a great deal more work, though, as before, a certain proportion of his labours was futile. Symonds was anxious that he should write an essay or essays on the Characters of Theophrastus, but *Treasure Island* was already beginning its serial course, with the latter half of it yet unwritten. Fortunately the inspiration that had failed the author returned, the last fourteen chapters took but a fortnight, and at the second wave the book was finished as easily as it was begun.

Again he started eagerly upon a new book, a *Life of Hazlitt*, he had long been wanting to write. There is a legend which is significant, although it cannot now be verified, that he had applied for a commission for this subject in some biographical series, but was refused on the ground that neither he nor his theme were of sufficient importance to justify their inclusion. Now he writes gleefully to his father: "I am in treaty with Bentley (Colvin again) for a Hazlitt! Is not that splendid? There will be piles of labour, but the book should be good. This will please you, will it not? Biography anyway, and a very interesting and sad one." He had long made a favourite study of the essays of his author, whose paper "On the Spirit of Obligations" had "been a turning-point" in his life. From no writer does he quote more freely, and he couples Hazlitt with Sterne and Heine as the best of companions on a walking tour. But a wider study of his writings produced a cooler feeling, and the *Liber Amoris* is said to have created a final distaste, which rendered any continued investigation or sympathetic treatment impossible.

Treasure Island, by "Captain George North," had been running an obscure career in the pages of its magazine from October to January, openly mocked at by more than one indignant reader. On its completion Stevenson announced to his father his intention of rewriting "the whole latter part, lightening and *siccating* throughout." But it did not make its appearance as a book till nearly two years later.

The Scottish history had fallen into abeyance, or had come down to an article on "Burt, Boswell, Mrs. Grant, and Scott," and a paper on the Glenure murder, afterwards the central incident in *Kidnapped*, but neither of these were even begun. The volume of *Familiar Studies* was prepared for press, and the critical preface was written. The two papers on Knox the author now found dull, and he even hesitated about keeping them back as material for a new life of the great Scottish statesman and Reformer.

About this time also he had a good deal of correspondence with Mr. Gosse on a work he had proposed they should undertake in collaboration — "a retelling, in choice literary form, of the most picturesque murder cases of the last hundred years. We were to visit the scenes of these crimes," says Mr. Gosse, "and turn over the evidence. The great thing, Louis said, was not to begin to write until we were thoroughly alarmed. 'These things must be done, my boy, under the very shudder of the goose-flesh.' We were to begin with the 'Story of the Red Barn,' which is indeed a tale pre-eminently worthy to be retold by Stevenson. But the scheme never came off, and is another of the dead leaves in his Vallombrosa." [1]

In January Stevenson gives an irresistible description of himself: "I dawdle on the balcony, read and write, and have fits of conscience and indigestion. The ingenious human mind, face to face with something it

[1] *Critical Kitcats*, p. 292.

231

downright ought to do, *does something else.* But the relief is temporary."

Temporary also was the idleness. *The Silverado Squatters,* the record of the circumstances of his honeymoon, was written, and no less than five magazine articles, including the first part of "Talk and Talkers" and the "Gossip on Romance." Still this did not satisfy him. He wrote to his mother: "I work, work away, and get nothing or but little done; it is slow, slow, slow; but I sit from four to five hours at it, and read all the rest of the time for Hazlitt." And to Charles Baxter, a little later, he wrote: "I am getting a slow, steady, sluggish stream of ink over paper, and shall do better this year than last." Before April he can say: "I have written something like thirty-five thousand words since I have been here, which shows at least I have been industrious." [1]

To this time apparently belong the verses called "The Celestial Surgeon," which are as characteristic of Stevenson as anything he ever wrote. An eloquent modern preacher, treating of the deadly sin of accidie, "gloom and sloth and irritation," the opposite of "the vertue that is called *fortitude* or strength," quotes these "graceful, noble lines" at length, and says, "Surely no poet of the present day, and none, perhaps, since Dante, has so truly told of the inner character of accidie, or touched more skilfully the secret of its sinfulness." [2]

Whether in spite or in consequence of his harder

[1] Cf. *Letters,* i. 237.

[2] The Right Rev. Dr. Paget, Bishop of Oxford. *The Spirit of Discipline,* Longmans, Green & Co., London, 1891.

work, his health continued to improve, notwithstanding great anxiety about his wife, who was affected by the high elevation. Early in December she was sent to Zürich and then to Berne, with indifferent results. Finally, Stevenson went down and brought her home on Christmas Day, the party travelling seven hours in an open sleigh in the snow, but fortunately nobody was the worse. Though frequently ailing, she managed with two short changes to stay out the necessary season, but was fit for little, and quite unable to take charge of the house. To cheer her depression, Symonds and her husband, and sometimes Mr. Horatio Brown, would forego their walk and spend the afternoon at her bedside. Stevenson would fling himself upon the bed with his feet to the pillow, and the hours passed in the most animated and varied discussion. Symonds, it will be remembered, was the Opalstein of "Talk and Talkers." On the first reading of that essay he affected indignation: "Louis Stevenson, what do you mean by describing me as a moonlight serenader?" The sketch, however, gives, I believe, a real impression of the qualities of his talk, and it is only to be regretted that he has nowhere done the same for his companion.

Housekeeping was a burden and a doubtful economy, but the châlet in other respects was a great success. For one thing, it got the sun an hour sooner, and kept it an hour later than the hotels; for another, it provided its master with a spot where he was at liberty to create and develop for himself the amusement which pleased him best of all — the game of war. His childish enthusiasm about the army in the Crimea will be

remembered, though it was but the common feeling of
the children of this country at the time.   Deeds of arms
would always raise a thrill in his breast, but so far as I
know there was no outward sign of this interest in
warfare or strategy during his youth or early manhood.
In December, 1878, he wrote from the Savile Club: "I
am in such glee about Peiwar.[1]   I declared yesterday I
was going to add the name to mine, and be Mr. Peiwar
Stevenson for the future."   In October, 1880, an old
general who was a friend of the family came to see
him in London, and brought as a present Sir Edward
Hamley's *Operations of War*.   R. A. M. Stevenson
was there at the time, and both cousins were trans-
ported with enthusiasm.   "I am drowned in it a
thousand fathom deep," wrote Louis, "and 'O that I
had been a soldier' is still my cry."   He had never
made any affectation of abandoning a pursuit he was
supposed to have outgrown.   He clung to the colour-
ing of prints and to childish paintings long after most
boys of his age have given up the diversions of the
nursery.   A large part of the winter of 1877 he spent
in building with toy-bricks in his room at Heriot Row,
and regretted that he had not been an architect.   As
Bishop Earle said of a child, "We laugh at his foolish
sports, but his game is our earnest": it often is not
wisdom, but dulness, that keeps men from joining in
the livelier fancies of children.   Stevenson, deterred by
no false shame, extracted from toys much of the zest
of reality, and raised their employment almost to the
intensity of active life.   And now, beginning to help
his schoolboy with games, he became absorbed in the

[1] Lord Roberts's brilliant victory over the Afghans.

pursuit, and developed a *kriegspiel* of his own, adapted
to the conditions under which, of necessity, he played.
While it was impossible for him to secure the services
of an umpire, this very independence allowed the operations to be protracted for any length of time needed for
the completion of an entire campaign. But his enthusiasm and the thoroughness and ingenuity he exhibited
are best described in the account given by his adversary,
Mr. Lloyd Osbourne:—

"The abiding spirit of the child in him was seldom
shown in more lively fashion than during those days of
exile at Davos, where he brought a boy's eagerness, a
man's intellect, a novelist's imagination, into the varied
business of my holiday hours; the printing-press, the
toy-theatre, the tin soldiers, all engaged his attention.
Of these, however, the tin soldiers most took his fancy;
and the war game was constantly improved and elab-
orated, until, from a few hours, a 'war' took weeks
to play, and the critical operations in the attic monop-
olised half our thoughts. This attic was a most chilly
and dismal spot, reached by a crazy ladder, and unlit
save for a single frosted window; so low at the eaves
and so dark that we could seldom stand upright, nor
see without a candle. Upon the attic floor a map was
roughly drawn in chalks of different colours, with
mountains, rivers, towns, bridges, and roads of two
classes. Here we would play by the hour, with tingling fingers and stiffening knees, and an intentness,
zest, and excitement that I shall never forget. The
mimic battalions marched and counter-marched,
changed by measured evolutions from column forma-
tion into line, with cavalry screens in front and massed

supports behind, in the most approved military fashion of to-day. It was war in miniature, even to the making and destruction of bridges, the intrenching of camps; good and bad weather, with corresponding influence on the roads; siege and horse artillery, proportionately slow, as compared to the speed of unimpeded foot, and proportionately expensive in the upkeep; and an exacting commissariat added the last touch of verisimilitude. Four men formed the regiment, or unit, and our shots were in proportion to our units and amount of our ammunition. The troops carried carts of printers' 'ems'—twenty 'ems' to each cart—and for every shot taken an 'em' had to be paid into the base, from which fresh supplies could be slowly drawn in empty carts returned for the purpose." [1]

The strength of the enemy in any given spot could only be ascertained according to strictly defined regulations, and an attempt was even made to mark certain districts as unhealthy and to settle by the hazard of the dice-box the losses incurred by all troops passing through them.

During one war Stevenson chronicled the operations in a series of extracts from the *Glendarule Times* and the *Yallobally Record*, until the editor of the latter sheet was hanged by order of General Osbourne and its place supplied by the less offensive *Herald*.

Year after year he reverted to the game, and even in Samoa there was a campaign room with the map coloured on the floor, although the painful realities of actual warfare, either present or imminent, occupied all our thoughts for the closing period of Stevenson's life.

[1] *Scribner's Magazine*, December, 1898, p. 709.

But busy as he was this winter, he had time not only for this game, but also, turning aside to help young Osbourne with his printing, he first wrote verses for the toy-press, and then, getting hold of a bit of rough wood, began to design and cut illustrations for his text, or in some cases to create pictures which a text must elucidate.

In February, 1882, he sent to his parents "two wood-cuts of my own cutting; they are moral emblems; one represents 'anger,' the other 'pride scorning poverty.' They will appear among others, accompanied by verses, in my new work published by S. L. Osbourne. If my father does not enjoy these, he is no true man." And to his mother: "Wood-engraving has suddenly drave between me and the sun. I dote on wood-engraving. I'm a made man for life. I've an amusement at last."

Of these blocks about two dozen in all were cut, most of them by Stevenson's own hands, though the elephant, at any rate, was due to his wife, and "the sacred ibis in the distance" was merely the result of an accident turned to advantage. He had in his boyhood received a few lessons in drawing as a polite accomplishment: later he found great difficulty in the mechanical work of his original profession, in which of course he had been specially trained. Thus, in 1868, he wrote to his mother, "It is awful how slowly I draw and how ill." Barbizon seemed to rouse in him no tendency to express himself in line or colour, and it was not till he was alone at Monastier in 1878 that he made for his own pleasure such sketches as any grown man with no technical education might attempt.

Art criticism is for the expert; I will only say that to

237

me these sketches seem to show an excellent eye for the configuration of the country. But after this Stevenson seems to have drawn no more landscape until, his camera being lost, he tried his hand at representing some of the coast scenery in the Marquesas, and his sketch, redrawn by Mr. Charles Wyllie, gives me a very vivid impression of the scenery of an island I have never visited.

It would be very easy to overrate not merely the importance but even the interest of these blocks. Stevenson soon obtained some pear-wood, and then, after he returned to Scotland, he procured box; on this latter material the illustrations of *The Graver and the Pen* were cut, but their merits are impaired rather than heightened by the improved technique.

That Stevenson had an eye for country, as I have said, for clouds, for water, and for the action of the human figure, the cuts are a clear proof. The most ridiculous of his puppets are full of life, from the " industrious pirate" with his spyglass, to Robin " who has that Abbot stuck as the red hunter spears the buck." One and all, they show in their rough state a touch full of spirit and original quality, that teaching might have refined away.[1]

In April again the family quitted the Alps, but this year with welcome news. " We now leave Davos for good, I trust, Dr. Ruedi giving me leave to live in France, fifteen miles as the crow flies from the sea, and if possible near a fir wood. This is a great blessing: I hope I am grateful."

[1] *The Studio*, Winter Number, 1896–97. Robert Louis Stevenson, Illustrator. By Joseph Pennell. With twelve illustrations.

They crossed the Channel with little delay; Louis stayed first at Weybridge, and then at Burford Bridge, where he renewed his friendship with Mr. George Meredith. By May 20th he was in Edinburgh, and there spent most of June, though he made a week's expedition with his father to Lochearnhead, hard by the Braes of Balquhidder. Here he made inquiries about the Appin murder, perpetrated only forty miles away, and was successful in finding some local traditions about the murderer still extant.[1]

The flow of work at the beginning of the year was followed by a long period of unproductiveness after he returned to this country. He had an article in each number of the *Cornhill* from April to August, but except the second part of "Talk and Talkers" these had been written at Davos. After this his connection with the magazine came to an end. During the past seven years its readers had grown accustomed to look eagerly every month in hope of finding an article by R. L. S., and all its rivals have, by comparison, ever since seemed conventional and dull. Mr. Leslie Stephen resigned the editorship in 1883 to the late James Payn, who was no less a friend of Stevenson and an admirer of his work, but the price of the magazine was reduced and its character somewhat modified. In August the *New Arabian Nights*, long withheld by the advice of an experienced publisher, were issued in two volumes by Messrs. Chatto & Windus, and reached a second edition before the end of the year.

On June 26th the family went to the manse of Stobo in Peeblesshire for the summer. But the weather was

[1] Introduction to *Kidnapped*.

bad, the house shut in by trees, and the result most unbeneficial. In a fortnight Louis was ordered away, went to London to consult Dr. Andrew Clark, and in accordance with his advice started on July 22nd for Speyside in the company of Mr. Colvin. The rest of the family soon joined him at Kingussie, and here again by a burn— "the golden burn that pours and sulks" [1]— he spent the last entire month he ever passed in Scotland. Having gone to France to write about Edinburgh, in the Highlands he turned again to France, and now wrote most of *The Treasure of Franchard*. The weather again did its worst; he had an invitation to meet Cluny Macpherson, and was eagerly looking forward to a talk about the Highlands. But a hemorrhage intervened, Stevenson had to leave in haste, and by September 9th he was in London, again asking the advice of Dr. Clark. The opinion was so far favourable that there was no need to return to Davos, which disagreed with Mrs. Stevenson, and of which they were both heartily tired. They were thus at liberty to seek a home in some more congenial spot.

[1] *Memories and Portraits*, p. 145.

CHAPTER X

" Happy (said I), I was only happy once, that was at Hyères; it came to end from a variety of reasons, decline of health, change of place, increase of money, age with his stealing steps; since then, as before then, I know not what it means."—*Vailima Letters*, p. 53.

ACCORDINGLY about the middle of September Stevenson started for the South of France, and since he was unfit to go alone, and his wife was too ill to undertake the journey, he started in the charge and company of his cousin, R. A. M. Stevenson.   Their object was to discover some place suitable for both husband and wife, possessing more of the advantages of a town and fewer of the drawbacks of a health-resort than the Alpine valley from which they were now finally released.   Paris was left without delay, and Montpellier was next tried and rejected, but not until Louis had a slight hemorrhage.   He wrote to his wife: "I spent a very pleasant afternoon in the doctor's consulting-room among the curious, meridional peasants, who quarrelled and told their complaints.   I made myself very popular there, I don't know how."

His companion had to return home, and Louis made his way to Marseilles, where, a few days later, on October 11th, he was joined by his wife.

No time was wasted; within three days a house that seemed all they could desire was found and taken.   It was a commodious *maison de campagne* with a large garden, situated about five miles from Marseilles, with such facilities of communication with the city as a considerable suburb ensures. "In a lovely spot, among lovely wooded and cliffy hills — most mountainous in line — far lovelier to my eyes than any Alps."

In another week they were installed in Campagne Defli, and had sent for such property as they needed. Here they proposed to make their home for several years. "The tragic folly of my summers is at an end for me," Louis wrote; "twice have I gone home and escaped with a flea in my ear; the third or fourth time I should leave my bones with a general verdict of 'sarve him right for a fool.'" "The white cliffs of Albion shall not see me," he wrote in January; "I am sick of relapsing; I want to ge twell." "As for my living in England, three years hence will be early enough to talk of it."

But whether the house or the neighbourhood or the season was unhealthy, St. Marcel proved a most unfortunate choice. Stevenson was never well there, and never for more than three or four days at a time capable of any work. He had several slight hemorrhages and mended very slowly. By Christmas he wrote: "I had to give up wood-engraving, chess, latterly even patience, and could read almost nothing but newspapers. It was dull but necessary. I seem hopelessly hidebound, as you see; nothing comes out of me but chips."

At the end of the year an epidemic of fever broke out in St. Marcel, and he found himself so unwell, that in desperation he went to Nice lest he should become too ill to move. They were unprepared for the move, and his wife stayed behind until they could obtain further supplies.   In the meantime telegrams and letters went astray, and at the end of a week Mrs. Stevenson arrived at Nice quite distraught.   She had received no news whatever of her husband, having telegraphed in all directions for three days in vain, and had been assured by every one that he must have had a fresh hemorrhage, have left the train at some wayside station, and there died and been buried.

In the meantime all went well, but it was obviously impossible for Stevenson to think of returning to St. Marcel; by the middle of February, 1883, they got the Campagne Defli off their hands, and were at liberty to seek a fresh settlement.   They thought of Geneva, but, after a short visit to Marseilles, they went to a hotel at Hyères, and there by the end of March were once more established in a house of their own — Châlet La Solitude.   It was situated just above the town, on a slope of the hill on which the castle stands, commanding a view of Les Oiseaux and the Îles d'Or; a cottage scarce as large as the Davos châlet, " with a garden like a fairy-story and a view like a classical landscape."

Here for a year, or, to be strictly accurate, for a little more than nine months, Stevenson was to find happiness, a greater happiness than ever came to him again, except perhaps at moments in his exile.   Hardly anything seemed wanting; his wife was always able to be with him, and he had besides the company of his stepson, in which he delighted.   There was the affectionate intercourse with his parents, clouded only by the gradual failure in his father's spirits; there was the correspondence with his friends; already in March he had been able to welcome Mr. Colvin as the first of his visitors;

and, not least, he found a measure of health once more and a renewed capacity for employing his increased skill.

Of the first of these elements in his happiness he wrote to his mother in 1884: "My wife is in pretty good feather; I love her better than ever and admire her more; and I cannot think what I have done to deserve so good a gift. This sudden remark came out of my pen; it is not like me; but in case you did not know, I may as well tell you, that my marriage has been the most successful in the world. I say so, and being the child of my parents, I can speak with knowledge. She is everything to me: wife, brother, sister, daughter and dear companion; and I would not change to get a goddess or a saint. So far, after four years of matrimony." And of his delight in his surroundings he said in 1883: "This house and garden of ours still seem to go between us and our wits." Their material comfort was further increased in May when Valentine Roch entered their service, an extremely clever and capable French girl, who remained with them for six years, and even accompanied them on their first cruise in the Pacific.

For a period of nearly eight months he had been unable to earn any money or to carry any work to a conclusion, and it was therefore with the greatest delight that in the beginning of May he received an offer from Messrs. Cassell for the book-rights of *Treasure Island*. "How much do you suppose? I believe it would be an excellent jest to keep the answer till my next letter. For two cents I would do so. Shall I? Anyway I'll turn the page first. No — well, a hundred pounds, all alive, O! A hundred jingling, tingling, golden, minted quid. Is not this wonderful? . . . It is dreadful to be a great, big man, and not to be able to buy bread." [1]

Already, before he reached La Solitude, his enforced leisure had come to an end. Verse-writing with him was almost always a resource of illness or of convalescence, and he now took advantage of his recovery to increase the poems of childhood (for which his first name was *Penny Whistles*), until they amounted to some eight-and-forty numbers. Now also in answer to an application from Mr. Gilder, the editor of the *Century Magazine*, *The Silverado Squatters* was finished and despatched to New York, and so began his first important connection with any of the American publishers who were afterwards to prove so lucrative to him. Of course, like others, he had suffered at the hands of persons who had not only appropriated his books without licence, but even, a less usual outrage, had wantonly misspelt his name. "I saw my name advertised in a number of the *Critic* as the work of one R. L. Stephenson; and, I own, I boiled. It is so easy to know the name of the man whose book you have stolen; for there it is, at full length, on the title-page of your booty. But no, damn him, not he! He calls me Stephenson." [2]

The ground was now clear before him, and on April 10th he set to work once more from the beginning upon *Prince Otto*, which he had left untouched for three years. Ten days later he wrote: "I am up to the waist in a story; a kind of one-volume novel; how do they ever puff them out into three? Lots of things happen in this thing of mine, and one volume will

[1] This was only payment in advance. The book in England has since brought the author and his representatives about two thousand pounds.

[2] *Letters*, i. 293.

swallow it without a strain." At first all went swimmingly. By May 5th—in five-and-twenty days—he had drafted fifteen chapters. But there was a stumbling-block in his path—he had yet to reckon with his women characters. When he came to the scenes where the intervention of the Countess von Rosen is described, his resources were taxed to their utmost, and when the battle went against him, he renewed his attack again and again. Seven times was the fifteenth chapter now rewritten, and it was only the eighth version which finally was suffered to pass.

On May 26th, in answer to Mr. Henderson's application for another story, he began *The Black Arrow*, and the first six chapters seem to have been finished in as many days. Eight years before, in studying the fifteenth century, he had read the Paston Letters, and mainly from this material he now constructed a style and story which he thought would please the public for whom he was writing, though to his friends he announced it with cynicism and described the work as "Tushery." On June 30th the first number of the tale appeared in *Young Folks;* for the next four months it continued with perfect regularity, and it was probably the one of its author's works which suffered most from the demands of periodical publication. In June he went for a week to Marseilles, and on July 1st left for Royat, and by these moves being separated from the instalments of his proof-sheets, he had at one time, according to his own account in later days, actually forgotten what had last happened to several of his principal characters. This, however, did not affect the popularity of the story, which, published like

Treasure Island under the signature of "Captain George North," had a vogue far beyond that of its predecessor, even raising the circulation of its paper by many hundreds of copies a week during its appearance. [1]

The visit to Royat was most successful, as his parents joined the party and there spent several weeks, but early in September Louis and his wife were back at La Solitude. *Treasure Island* had been prepared for press, and was already in the hands of the printers with the sole exception of the chart out of which the story had grown. This, having been accidentally mislaid, had now to be reconstructed from the text, and was being drawn in the Stevensons' office in Edinburgh. In spite of what had been said about rewriting and improving the story, only a few paragraphs were altered, chiefly in the sixteenth and two following chapters, and none of the modifications were of any importance. [2]

On September 19th Stevenson heard of the death of his old friend Walter Ferrier, who had long been in bad health, but was not supposed to be in any immediate danger. The record of their friendship is contained in the essay called "Old Mortality," which was written this winter; part of the letter has already been quoted [3] which Stevenson wrote to Mr. Henley at this time upon hearing of their common loss, a letter which is, moreover, given at length in Mr. Colvin's collection. Hence there is no occasion to say more than that

[1] The *Academy*, 3rd March, 1900.
[2] Cf. the *Academy*, 3rd March, 1900.
[3] P. 106.

this was the first breach death had made in the inner circle of Stevenson's friends.

That very spring he had written in a letter of consolation, "I am like a blind man in speaking of these things, for I have never known what mourning is, and the state of my health permits me to hope that I shall carry this good fortune unbroken to the grave." The hope was not to be fulfilled, but never again, with the exception of his father and of Fleeming Jenkin, did any loss throughout his life so nearly affect him as the death of Walter Ferrier.

At once his thoughts turned to the past, the past that was, and that which might have been; and he again took up the fragment which he had written upon "Lay Morals" in the spring of 1879. On October 2nd he wrote to his father:—

"This curious affair of Ferrier's death has sent me back on our relation and my past with much unavailing wonder and regret. Truly, we are led by strange paths. A feeling of that which lacked with Ferrier and me when we were lads together has put me upon a task which I hope will not be disliked by you: a sketch of some of the more obvious provinces and truths of life for the use of young men. The difficulty and delicacy of the task cannot be exaggerated. Here is a fine opportunity to pray for me: that I may lead none into evil. I am shy of it; yet remembering how easy it would have been to help my dear Walter and me, had any one gone the right way about, spurs me to attempt it. I will try to be honest, and then there can be no harm, I am assured; but I say again: a fine opportunity to pray for me. Lord, defend me from all idle conformity to please the face of man; from all display, to catch applause; from all bias of my own evil; in the name of Christ. Amen."

Nevertheless he made but little more progress with his Ethics. After a new preface addressed "to any young man, conscious of his youth, conscious of vague powers and qualities, and fretting at the bars of life," he reverted to his earlier manuscript, which still remains the more effective of the two drafts.

In October he received an offer from America for a book upon the islands of the Grecian Archipelago; but in consideration of the risk involved, and of the expenses of the journey, he fortunately decided not to accept the proposal.

All through the autumn his house continued to afford him fresh satisfaction. "My address is still the same," he writes to Mr. Low,[1] "and I live in a most sweet corner of the universe, sea and fine hills before me, and a rich variegated plain; and at my back a craggy hill, loaded with vast feudal ruins. I am very quiet; a person passing by my door half startles me; but I enjoy the most aromatic airs, and at night the most wonderful view into a moonlit garden. By day this garden fades into nothing, overpowered by its surroundings and the luminous distance; but at night, and when the moon is out, that garden, the arbour, the flight of stairs that mount the artificial hillock, the plumed blue gum-trees that hang trembling, become the very skirts of Paradise. Angels I know frequent it; and it thrills all night with the flutes of silence."

This enchanting abode and the excellence of the

[1] *Letters*, i. 287.

climate were to Stevenson the chief recommendations of Hyères, for of the residents and of the outside country he saw little or nothing, restricting himself to his own house and almost entirely to the circle of his own household. It was in the days of Fontainebleau and of the journeys that he acquired his knowledge of France and its inhabitants, to whatever use he may afterwards have turned them; but his immediate surroundings for the time seldom affected his work. And few foreigners have shown such understanding as is to be found in the stories of *The Treasure of Franchard* and *Providence and the Guitar*.

It is to this period that the reminiscence belongs, recorded in his letter to Mr. W. B. Yeats, of the spell cast upon him by Meredith's *Love in a Valley;* "the stanzas beginning 'When her mother tends her' haunted me and made me drunk like wine; and I remember waking with them all the echoes of the hills about Hyères." [1]

He began a story called *The Travelling Companion*, afterwards refused by a publisher as "a work of genius but indecent," and two years later condemned by Stevenson as having "no urbanity and glee, and no true tragedy"; later still it was burned on the ground that "it was not a work of genius, and *Jekyll* had supplanted it." The *Note on Realism* was written for the *Magazine of Art*, and *Prince Otto*, by the beginning of December, was wanting only the last two chapters. And at the end of this year or the beginning of next the copyright of his first three books was bought back from the publishers by his father. The *Donkey* had

---

[1] *Letters*, ii. 324.

gone into a third edition, the *Voyage* into a second; of the essays only nine hundred copies had been sold, and so badly were all three selling that the price was no more than a hundred pounds.

Treasure Island was published as a book in the end of November, when Stevenson obtained his first popular success. Its reception reads like a fairy-tale. Statesmen and judges and all sorts of staid and sober men became boys once more, sitting up long after bedtime to read their new book. The story goes that Mr. Gladstone got a glimpse of it at a colleague's house, and spent the next day hunting over London for a second-hand copy. The editor of the *Saturday Review*, the superior, cynical "Saturday" of old days, wrote excitedly to say that he thought *Treasure Island* was the best book that had appeared since *Robinson Crusoe;* and James Payn, who, if not a great novelist himself, yet held an undisputed position among novelists and critics, sent a note hardly less enthusiastic. Mr. Andrew Lang spent over it "several hours of unmingled bliss." "This is the kind of stuff a fellow wants. I don't know, except *Tom Sawyer* and the *Odyssey*, that I ever liked any romance so well." It was translated and pirated in all directions, appearing within a couple of years as a *feuilleton* even in Greek and Spanish papers. For all this, it brought no very great emolument, for during its first twelve months no more than five thousand six hundred copies were sold in Great Britain.

Its author, at all events, did not lose his head or overestimate his merits. Writing to his parents, he says: "This gives one strange thoughts of how very bad the common run of books must be; and generally all the books that the wiseacres think too bad to print are the very ones that bring me praise and pudding."

One link with the past had snapped, one friendship had vanished, and Stevenson was looking forward all the more eagerly to seeing two of his oldest friends, Mr. Henley and Mr. Baxter, who were coming out to spend a long-promised holiday with him. Before it could begin, *Prince Otto* ought to be finished, and to this end he devoted all his powers. The New Year came, his friends arrived at Hyères, and for about a week he enjoyed the delights to which he had looked forward. But the house was too small for their reception, and Stevenson proposed that they should all go away together to some other place, that he might share with them the benefit of a change. Accordingly the party of four went to Nice, and there almost at once Stevenson took cold. At first it seemed slight, and his friends, who were due to return home, went away without thought of anxiety. The cold, however, resulted in congestion of the lungs, and suddenly the situation became grave. "At a consultation of doctors," Mrs. Stevenson says, "I was told there was no hope, and I had better send for some member of the family to be with me at the end. Bob Stevenson came, and I can never be grateful enough for what he did for me then. He helped me to nurse Louis, and he kept me from despair as I believe no one else could have done; he inspired me with hope when there seemed no hope."

Very slowly he grew better; it was some time before he was out of danger, and a month before he was able to set foot outside the house; but at last they returned to La Solitude. Before his return he wrote in answer to his mother's inquiries: "I survived where a stronger man would not. There were never two opinions as to my immediate danger; of course it was chuck-farthing for my life. That is over, and I have only weakness to contend against. . . . Z——told me to leave off wine, to regard myself as 'an old man,' and to 'sit by my fire.' None of which I wish to do. . . . As for my general health, as for my consumption, we can learn nothing till Vidal[1] sees me, but I believe the harm is little, my lungs are so tough."

This illness, however, marked the beginning of a new and protracted period of ill-health, which lasted with but little intermission until he had left Europe.

Miss Ferrier, his friend's sister, came out at this time and stayed with them until their return to England, proving an unfailing support to them in their increasing troubles. For in the first week in May Stevenson was attacked with the most violent and dangerous hemorrhage he ever experienced. It occurred late at night, but in a moment his wife was by his side. Being choked with the flow of blood and unable to speak, he made signs to her for a paper and pencil, and wrote in a neat firm hand, "Don't be frightened; if this is death, it is an easy one." Mrs. Stevenson had always a small bottle of ergotin and a minim-glass in readiness; these she brought in order to administer the prescribed quantity. Seeing her alarm, he took bottle and glass away from her, measured the dose correctly with a perfectly steady hand, and gave the things back to her with a reassuring smile.

Recovery was very slow and attended by numerous

[1] His own extremely clever doctor at Hyères.

complications, less dangerous, but even more painful than the original malady. The dust of street refuse gave him Egyptian ophthalmia, and sciatica descending upon him caused him the more pain, as he was suffering already from restlessness. The hemorrhage was not yet healed, and we now hear for the first time of the injunctions to absolute silence, orders patiently obeyed, distasteful as they were. In silence and the dark, and in acute suffering, he was still cheery and undaunted. When the ophthalmia began and the doctor first announced his diagnosis, Mrs. Stevenson felt that it was more than any one could be expected to bear, and went into another room, and there, in her own phrase, "sat and gloomed." Louis rang his bell and she went to him, saying, in the bitterness of her spirit, as she entered the room, "Well, I suppose that this is the very best thing that could have happened!" "Why, how odd!" wrote Louis on a piece of paper, "I was just going to say those very words." When darkness fell upon him and silence was imposed, and his right arm was in a sling on account of the hemorrhage, his wife used to amuse him for part of the day by making up tales, some of which they afterwards used in the *Dynamiter;* when these were at an end, he continued the *Child's Garden,* writing down the new verses for himself in the dim light with his left hand. And at this time he wrote the best of all his poems, the "Requiem" beginning "Under the wide and starry sky," which ten years later was to mark his grave upon the lonely hill-top in Samoa.

When he got a little better he wrote to his mother, "I do nothing but play patience and write verse, the true sign of my decadence. With careful nursing he began to mend. Here, as everywhere, he excited the utmost sympathy, which manifested itself sometimes in embarrassing and unexpected ways. "The washer-woman's little boy brought, of all things in the world, a canary to amuse the sick gentleman! Fortunately it does n't sing, or it would drive the sick gentleman mad."

Thomas Stevenson was in too precarious health even to be told of his son's illness, but the two friends who had visited Louis at Nice in January took counsel and on their own responsibility sent their doctor from London to see what could be done, and at any rate to learn the exact condition of the patient. In a few days Mrs. Stevenson was able to write to her mother-in-law:—

"[*18th May, 1884.*] — . . . The doctor says, 'Keep him alive till he is forty, and then although a winged bird, he may live to ninety.' But between now and forty he must live as though he were walking on eggs, and for the next two years, no matter how well he feels, he must live the life of an invalid. He must be perfectly tranquil, trouble about nothing, have no shocks or surprises, not even pleasant ones; must not eat too much, drink too much, laugh too much; may write a little, but not too much; talk *very* little, and walk no more than can be helped."

His recovery was steady and satisfactory; with great caution and by the aid of a courier the party made their way to Royat without mishap early in June. For a moment Stevenson turned his thoughts reluctantly towards Davos, and then wrote to his mother announcing his return to England in order to obtain a final medical opinion upon his health and prospects. The only

course before him apparently was to "live the life of a
delicate girl" until he was forty. But uncongenial as
this seemed, his spirits were as high as ever, and he
signed the letter with a string of names worthy of
Bunyan's own invention—"I am, yours,

Mr. Muddler.
Mr. Addlehead.
Mr. Wandering Butterwits.
Mr. Shiftless Inconsistency.
Sir Indecision Contentment."

The journey was safely accomplished, and Stevenson
and his wife reached England on the 1st of July, the day
before the first representation on the London stage of
Deacon Brodie.